Arthur C. Clarke

A Life Remembered

by

Fred Clarke

with

Mark Stewart, Kelvin F. Long
and
Robert Godwin

Foreword by Gregory Benford

And a special introduction by Angie Edwards

A Publication of Apogee Prime in conjunction with The British Interplanetary Society

© 2013 Apogee Prime/BIS

Apogee Prime, a Division of Griffin Media, Burlington Ontario, Canada, L7R 2B5

http://www.apogeeprime.com

The British Interplanetary Society , 27-29 South Lambeth Road, London, SW8 1SZ,

Tel.+44 (0) 20 7735 3160, Fax: +44 (0) 20 7587 5118, www.bis-space.com.

ISBN 978-1-926837-26-0

Front Cover Art by David A. Hardy & Anthony Naylor.

All images Apogee Prime,BIS or Clarke family unless noted

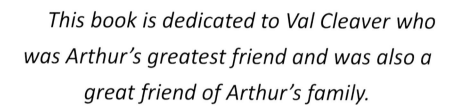

This book is dedicated to Val Cleaver who was Arthur's greatest friend and was also a great friend of Arthur's family.

"*Without visionaries like Arthur Clarke there would be no British Interplanetary Society*"

Suszann Parry, Executive Secretary, BIS

Contents

Acknowledgements   7

Foreword by Gregory Benford: Remembering Arthur   9

Preface by the Authors   13

Special Introduction by Angie Edwards   15

Chapter I. Childhood

    Vignettes by Fred Clarke   17

Chapter II. Early Days

    The Road from Ego to Fame by Robert Godwin   43

    Science Fiction – Past, Present and Future by Arthur C. Clarke   87

    The British Fan in his Natural Haunts - Arthur Clarke by William F. Temple   90

    The British Fan - William F. Temple by Arthur C. Clarke   95

Chapter III. Friends and Followers

    Arthur C. Clarke: a Friend to Love and Admire by Frederick I Ordway III   101

    Arthur C. Clarke by Michael Moorcock   103

    Arthur C. Clarke by Ben Bova   106

    The Sentinel by Keir Dullea   107

    Arthur C. Clarke by Robert J. Sawyer   108

Chapter IV. The Clarke Legacy

    An Interview with Fred Clarke   111

Chapter V. Tales from Taprobane

    An Interview with Nalaka Gunawardene   117

    Rendezvous with Arthur by Michael Lennick   128

    The Brightest Star by Helen Sharman   133

Chapter VI. Remembering Arthur

    Members of the British Interplanetary Society reminisce   135

      Stephen Baxter, Martin Fry, David A. Hardy, Mat Irvine, Bert Lewis,

      Kelvin F. Long, Sir Patrick Moore, Ray Ward, David Baker.

Chapter VII. Treading the Sands of Mars: Arthur's Work in Retrospect

    The City and the Stars by Kelvin F. Long   147

    The Sands of Mars by John Silvester   149

    The Sands of Mars by Adam Crowl   150

    Childhood's End by Gregory L. Matloff   151

    Rendezvous With Rama by Paul McAuley   153

    Earthlight by Adam Crowl   155

    2001: A Space Odyssey by Mark Stewart   156

    Growing Up: Childhood Ends by Andy Sawyer   159

    Arthur's Guide to the Universe by Mark Stewart   162

Chapter VIII. Old Spaceship

    The Spaceship by Kelvin F. Long   167

    Blueprints for a Starship by Stephen Baxter   170

    Creating a Self-Fulfilling Prophecy in Space by Kelvin F. Long   179

Chapter IX. The Father to the Man by Stephen Baxter   185

Chapter X. Interplanetary Men: Arthur Clarke and Olaf Stapledon

    Cosmic visionaries by Mark Stewart   193

Chapter XI. Before The Odyssey by Kelvin F. Long   199

Chapter XII Beyond 2001 - The Gala by Robert Godwin   205

Chapter XIII. Later days, 90th Birthday Reflections by Sir Arthur C. Clarke   219

Chapter XIV. Fred Clarke by Mark Stewart   223

Chapter XV. Fictional Last Word   225

Resources & Recommended Reading   226

Selected Papers by Arthur C. Clarke   227

About the Authors   228

Acknowledgements

Fred Clarke and the co-authors would like to acknowledge the kind assistance of several people during the construction of this text. Firstly, a huge thanks to the space artist David A. Hardy who produced the front cover, free of charge. The alignment of the Moon, Sun and Earth is a deliberate allusion to the story *2001: A Space Odyssey*. The elephant and bicycle depiction was produced by the cartoonist and caricaturist Anthony Naylor, based on one of the stories told in this book. Permission to use the *Astounding Stories* magazine cover from March 1930 was provided by Carol Demont and Abby Browning of Penny Publications LLC. Permission to use the *Amazing Stories* cover from November 1928 was provided, free of charge, by William Frank Engle, Administrator Frank R. Paul Estate and by Frank R. Paul's grandson Carol Engle, Executive Assistant, Frank R. Paul's Estate. Thanks to Andy Sawyer of the Science Fiction Library Special Collections Archive, University of Liverpool, for providing high quality copies of these images. Also to the Judith Merril Collection for archival help.

All extracts from Novae Terrae are presented here verbatim and are gratefully included with permission of the various estates. Thank you to John Davey for providing the photocopies from his own collection of this all-but-extinct and rare piece of Clarke/ BIS history. Thank you to Philip Turner, Anne and Joe Patrizio, Kevin and Alistair Mayer, Jill Godfrey, Rohan da Silva of the Arthur C. Clarke Family Trust, Amanda and Howard Burgess and Rob Hansen.

A thank you to all those who contributed to this book, including Stephen Baxter, Martin Fry, David Hardy, Mat Irvine, John Silvester, Adam Crowl, Michael Moorcock, Keir Dullea, Andy Sawyer, Bert Lewis, Sir Patrick Moore, Ben Bova, Ray Ward, David Baker, Fred Ordway, Robert Sawyer, Paul McAuley, Gregory Matloff, Helen Sharman and Nalaka Gunawardene. Thanks to the Richard Huish School for providing information. Thanks to Neil McAleer for giving general support to the project. A special thanks to Gregory Benford for writing the Foreword and Angie Edwards for writing the introduction. Grateful thanks are also extended to staff at The British Interplanetary Society, particularly Suszann Parry (Executive Secretary), Mary Todd and Ben Jones. Thanks also to BIS Council members Richard Osborne, Colin Philp, Alistair Scott and Bob Parkinson. Thanks to David A. Hardy and Stephen Ashworth for proof reading an earlier version of the book.

A loving thank you to Fred's two daughters, Angie Edwards and Dianne Skates, and their respective families. May this book throw a little more light on Arthur's life and the huge admiration he still attracts around the world.

Fred, Kelvin, Mark and Robert

Foreword

Remembering Arthur

by Gregory Benford

I first met him at the 1979 science fiction Worldcon in Brighton, though he had loomed in my life for decades before. Five minutes into our friendship he said amid the crowded convention floor, *"Let's go up to my room so we can think."* In the elevator he said he'd wanted to get away from the press of crowds, because he was feeling *"unsteady"* – first signs of the post-polio that would shadow his later life. So we sat in his hotel room and waxed on about the future, ideas, stories we loved. He saw the past as a guide, but what could come next filled him with wonder. In *Profiles of the Future* (1962), an elegantly phrased *Inquiry into the limits of the possible*, he balanced knowledge with his fictional side, exploring what might be achieved within the bounds of scientific law. Books on futurology date notoriously, yet this one has not, because Clarke was unafraid of being adventurous.

Talking to him, I recalled that back in 1962 Clarke foresaw that the mobile telephone would mean that no one could fully escape society, even at sea or on a mountaintop. He went on to describe huge electronic libraries, the breakdown of censorship and high definition electronic screens. He got almost all his many predictions right. About such ideas he was often wryly witty. I can hear in memory his quick darting mind, seen in his many aphorisms. On religion: *"I don't believe in God but I'm very interested in her."* Of space and politics: *"There is hopeful symbolism in the fact that flags do not wave in a vacuum."* On progress: *"New ideas pass through three periods: It can't be done; it probably can be done, but it's not worth doing; I knew it was a good idea all along!"* His vision carried precisely because he remained almost obliviously above the fray: *"Politics and economics are concerned with power and wealth, neither of which should be the primary, still less the exclusive, concern of full-grown men."* But speculation had to be rigorous. *"Exact knowledge is the friend, not the enemy, of imagination and fantasy."*

He was quite aware that his greatest success was his co-authorship with Stanley Kubrick of the film and novel, *2001: A Space Odyssey.* Its blend of hard technology and mystical opening was a huge cultural benchmark, bringing to life his assertion that *"whatever other perils humanity may face in the future that lies ahead, boredom is not among them."* Kubrick observed, *"He has the kind of mind of which the world can never have enough, an array of imagination, intelligence, knowledge and a quirky curiosity, which often uncovers more than the first three qualities."* Clarke later relished telling the story of visiting the United States when an immigration official looked at his passport and said, *"I won't let you in until you explain the ending of 2001. "*

From the 1980s he sometimes used a wheelchair but could still continue one of his lifelong passions, scuba diving. He founded the first diving shop in Asia, having moved permanently to Sri Lanka in 1956. He felt *"perfectly operational underwater"* and restored the business after the 2004 tsunami. I was to go diving with him in 1995 but the weather turned bad.

Sri Lanka gave Clarke creative isolation, but he became the first citizen of the global village, travelling and later keeping in touch with friends, colleagues and fans via daily e-mails. Surrounded by spicy tropical cuisine, he never gave up his taste for a steady diet of bland English food, preferring roast beef and Yorkshire pudding. I ate this dutifully in his home, and dined on local zippy curries the rest of the day, during my two visits to Sri Lanka.

In 2007 when we visited him again in Colombo, he seemed unsettled by the unending Tamil Tiger war. The fascist Tigers had been assassinating major public figures to draw attention; there were armed guards at both intersections by his home, and one near his driveway. Arthur hated small-mindedness, and the Tamils had come to haunt him. Luckily, they're gone now. Arthur didn't live to see their demise, alas.

He took us to the Swimming Club for lunch, a sunny ocean spot left over from the Raj. It felt somehow right to watch the Indian Ocean curl in, breaking on the rocks, and speak of space – the last, greatest ocean. Our hotel with a similar ocean view, the Galle Face, is the oldest grand Raj hotel east of Suez, dating from before the Civil War, and reeks of atmosphere. Since the Galle Face is next to the British High Commission compound, and just down the street from the Presidential residence, subtle security lurks everywhere. A heavy machine gun on a nearby tower peered over us as we swam in the pool. Arthur mused, "All this effort, all this death, when we could be building the staging area for a seaborne space elevator." In *The Fountains of Paradise* he had moved the island five degrees south so it could sit on the equator.

In his home's *"Ego Chamber,"* amid many awards, I noticed a page by Apollo 11 astronaut Neil Armstrong, saying, *"To Arthur – who visualized the nuances of lunar flying before I experienced them."* His last wishes were for the further expansion of human horizons, saying to the Mars Society, *"Whether we become a multi-planet species with unlimited horizons, or are forever confined to Earth, will be decided in the twenty-first century amid the vast plains, rugged canyons and lofty mountains of Mars."* It is easy to see him as a monument now, but he was more interesting as a man. That's what I miss most.

Elisabeth Benford, Arthur C. Clarke, Gregory Benford
Colombo (2007)

Preface

Why compile a book about the childhood and life of Arthur C. Clarke? Perhaps because that childhood, and the adult life which followed, inspired and encouraged so many other young minds to become involved in space. For many this fascination with space has proved to be a life-long interest and a source of fellowship with other "space cadets" of all ages, backgrounds and nationalities. Arthur's personal history and that of the British Interplanetary Society (BIS) are closely linked; the little boy that built experimental rockets on the family farm would one day give lectures on space travel to his fellow BIS members. It seemed to us fitting that this book should include the memories of some of those BIS members who knew Arthur and who were so clearly inspired and influenced by his presence within the Society. Hence the second half of this volume is largely devoted to those reminiscences, to the living testimony that is a fitting compliment to Fred's own recollections.

A desire to honour the Clarke legacy was certainly our motivation, in part at least, for working on this project, which has allowed us to bring Fred's memories to life and make them available to all Clarke fans everywhere. Fred and Arthur have been involved with the BIS since its founding days and even now it is impossible to be a member of the Society and not feel their presence, either when visiting the Society London headquarters or when reading any of its publications. The Clarke brothers continue to influence the Society in many ways, inspiring lectures and symposia which celebrate speculative thinking and ground-breaking discussions which linger in the mind long after the events are over. And then there is the undeniable lineage that links Arthur to modern-day science fiction writers such as Stephen Baxter, a fellow of the BIS and co-author with Arthur on several joint novels.

Through our collaboration on this project we had the great privilege of meeting Fred in person several times and experienced first-hand the vitality, generosity, optimism and sense of humour that was and is such a strong trait in both brothers and which runs through much of Arthur's writing. Perhaps no member of the BIS embodies the Society motto more than Arthur C. Clarke, whose own journey from imagination to reality resulted in so many wonderful works of fiction. That remarkable life story had its origins in Arthur's boyhood on the family farm at Ballifants in Somerset, where both brothers got up to plenty of benign mischief as Fred has so vividly recalled. For Arthur, it was the start of an odyssey that would one day reach out into space, all the way to the stars and beyond. Here then is a faithful and accurate depiction of those early days, of how the odyssey began. We hope you will enjoy the journey.

Fred, Mark, Kelvin and Robert

Arthur C. Clarke takes his first flight in an Avro 504. Nora Clarke is in the rear seat. Captain Percival Philips at the controls. Taunton circa 1927

Special Introduction

This is the first truly personal memoir of my Uncle Arthur that I can recall reading. Who better to have written it than Fred, who has really spent the best part of his adult life supporting and promoting his brother's life and works. Many of the stories are truly evocative, especially where they concern Ballifants, the farm which still belongs to our family, and where we spent so many wonderful family holidays. It is sometimes hard to remind ourselves that people of great fame and intellect come from perfectly normal backgrounds – well perhaps not so normal in this case – but certainly from a modest beginning. Arthur certainly did, which can give us all hope for the future.

Angie Edwards is the daughter of Fred Clarke and a Board Member of the Arthur C. Clarke Foundation

Arthur C. Clarke Official Birth Plaque in Minehead

Chapter I - Childhood

Vignettes

by Fred Clarke

Charles Clarke and Nora: A Courtship in Morse Code

Nora Willis lived with her sister and widowed mother in a large house in Blenheim Road, opposite Minehead's lovely Blenheim Gardens. She worked for the General Post Office and was very good at her job. In fact, she was often sent out to the sub-offices when they were short staffed, or their account books did not match up with their sales.

However, Nora's main job was operating the GPO's latest piece of technical equipment. This was the Morse recorder which was used to send urgent messages from offices all over the country. This was especially busy during the war years.

It was worked by operating a key that sent the dots and dashes for the Morse code to the recipient. This meant that both operators had to have a good knowledge of the Morse code. Between sending official messages there were often long gaps during which the operators used to chat to one another. Charles also worked as the Morse operator at Taunton Head Office and during these gaps he and Nora got to know each other; so well in fact that their entire courtship was carried out over the twenty five miles between their respective offices.

During this time Charles joined the Royal Engineers, was commissioned and sent to France. However, when he had a break he returned to Taunton, and would give his former mates a helping hand usually operating the Morse Machine. When Charles and Nora could get away together they would both cycle to the Blue Anchor and meet for tea. Nearby was the Camp of the Army Corps of Signals.

At one of their rendezvous they had just settled down for a meal when they heard a tapping from the far side of the tea room. This was followed by further tapping from the other side. They soon realised that the soldiers were commenting, in Morse Code, on the pretty young lady and the luck of the Officer escorting her. As they left at the end of their meal, while Charles was paying the bill, Nora picked up a spoon and saucer and tapped "Thank you," leaving the room in stunned silence! Charles and Nora were married at St Michaels Church on North Hill, very close to the new house to which her family had moved.

Ballifants – A Starter Farm for a Returning Hero

When Arthur's Father returned from France at the end of the Great War he was in a very poor physical condition. Despite this he and Nora decided to take up farming, which was probably the worst decision they could have made.

With a partner, they bought *Bethan*, a small farm near Chard, but Charles was unfit for any hard work. That meant they had to hire in labour for the heavy jobs like haymaking and harvesting, which greatly increased their expenses. After losing several animals, which they were unable to replace, they were completely bankrupt.

However, during the war the government had set up a number of small farms, known as Smallholdings, for the use of returning soldiers. These were carved out of big estates, whose owners had died in the war. These young men, the pride of British Manhood, had been called into the Forces, given the rank of Officer and then with a supreme lack of intelligence made to wear a leather over-belt, known as a Sam Browne. Of course the German snipers knew this, so the targets they went for first were the Officers, leaving the squads leaderless.

This left many great Estates with nobody left to run them, so the

Government bought them at knock down prices and divided them into hundred acre farms, with a homestead and some outbuildings. These starter farms were allocated to returning soldiers.

One such farm was the Lethbridge estate in Bishops Lydeard. This was Charles's own village, so he applied for one, and became the tenant of *Ballifants*. The farm consisted of a three hundred year-old, four bedroom stone built house, four fields of grass, one large arable field, an orchard and a walled garden. With what animals they had salvaged from their last adventure, Nora and Charles set up home there, together with their two sons: Arthur (born 16 December 1917) and Fred (born 7 April 1921). Their daughter Mary was born there four years later, followed by Michael, four years after that.

Obviously, life was a great struggle, especially for Nora, as Charles was confined to bed for much of the time, and finally died in Bristol Infirmary in 1931. Nora continued on her own, on a pension of ten shillings a week, feeding the family from the garden which she cultivated herself, and with chickens and eggs.

She made friends who helped with the heavy jobs, bought a couple of horses, and gave riding lessons which were very popular in those days of petrol shortage. She also took in paying guests, who would return year after year.

Nora attended to the birth of all her animals, and never lost a single one. In fact she built up a flock of sheep from neighbours' gifts of abandoned lambs. Gradually she built up a small bank balance and used this to buy a horse and trap, so when Arthur began to attend school a mile away in Bishops Lydeard she was able to drive him there.

Aunt Nellie and the West Somerset Railway

For much of his childhood Arthur had the choice of two very different environments. With his mother he had the healthy life of the farm; while with his grandmother he had the fun, liveliness and sands of the seaside town of Minehead.

Arthur at 4 Months Old, Blenheim Place

The young Arthur takes early steps with Mother Nora

*Arthur at Minehead
circa 1920*

*Arthur around five
or six years old with
a buddy*

These two environments were linked by the West Somerset Railway. If Arthur was ill, or bored with the animals, his mother would harness up the trap and take him down to Bishops Lydeard railway station, where she would hand him over to the guard of the next train.

When they got to Minehead the guard would hand him on to his Aunt Nellie, and when he wanted to go home, the reverse procedure would take place. These trips brought Arthur a lasting love of the West Somerset Railway which continued for the rest of his life.

Dodging Missiles in Blenheim Gardens

Another great link with Minehead was the Blenheim Gardens. These lovely gardens were right opposite the family home in Blenheim Road and were a wonderful play centre for young people. But they were always under the watchful eye of the head gardener. He had served in the Great War and on his return had left one leg in France! However, he was a match for any small boy he might find hiding in the shrubs. He would give them a start and if he found they were getting away from him, he would hurl his supporting stick after them. He had a deadly aim (Health and Safety Regulations had not been invented in those days.) It was good training for when Arthur was on the farm and was sent out to catch horses ready for his mother's riding lessons.

Family Debates and Skirmishes at the Kitchen Table

Very few people won in an argument with Arthur, except perhaps his mother; but then she had her own methods. His instant repartee was more than a match for most people, particularly for his brother and sister, and Arthur would often start an argument with them at the tea table, which could end in chaos.

When this happened, as it did quite often, Nora had her own way of dealing with it. In the garden was an apple tree which produced a number of long, floppy sticks which she could use to reach across the table. Nora used the sticks regularly and impartially to make her point and, in order to do so without delay, she kept a supply of them in a cupboard behind her. There was a pair of these cupboards, built into the kitchen wall at ceiling level each side of the kitchen cooker, well above the reach of enquiring hands.

One afternoon Arthur realised that his self-control would be unlikely to last throughout teatime, so with my assistance, he pushed the table below the cupboard with the sticks stacked in it. Then he put a chair on the table, and me on the chair! I was now able to reach the sticks, which I pulled out one at a time and which Arthur then placed into the fire. The fire burned brightly, which surprised Mother, but she said nothing, until the inevitable happened. She jumped to her feet and reached up into the stick store and came out with nothing. Without a moment's hesitation she reached into the other cupboard, brought out another stick – with others for spare – and set to work impartially on the two boys, as well as their sister, now having hysterics. That was an event which only ever happened once. That summer the tree mysteriously died and I had the great pleasure of cutting it down.

Arthur the School Teacher – at Eleven Years of Age!

Arthur's next school was Bishops Lydeard Primary School where he remained until he took his Eleven-Plus examination, to great effect, for it brought him a full scholarship to Richard Huish Grammar School in Taunton. Here again he excelled and was always in demand by other students, as he had the ability to break down complex problems into easily understood smaller problems.

The journey to Huish was about six miles, starting with a mile walk through the fields. This took him to the Lethbridge Arms, where the kindly landlady would allow the boys to sit in front of her entrance fire to warm themselves while they waited for the school bus.

The journey on the bus was a good opportunity for the other students to get Arthur to correct their homework before they got to school. This was a greatly appreciated service, but it ceased very suddenly when one of the masters, who lived in the village, had an accident with his car and started to take the bus instead. This resulted in a noticeable fall in the marks of the Bishop Lydeard contingent, which was never explained, though easily guessed.

Richard Huish Grammar School: Outsmarting the Overlords

Arthur was always a very fit young man. Living on the fat of the farm, mainly Somerset clotted cream, and with plenty of exercise – catching horses, collecting cattle and chopping wood for the fires – he felt he had all the exercise he required.

However Dr Arnold Goodliffe, the Headmaster of Huish School, had other ideas. He organized the class routines to include a sports afternoon every Thursday. There were certain disadvantages in this, one being that the Huish playing fields were right outside the town. That meant the youngsters had to change into their sports kit at the school and then walk the entire length of East Street and East Reach to the Hamilton Gault Playing fields, in single file.

Arthur himself did not approve of this wasted time, so he would attach himself to the end of the crocodile and as they were marching down the town, he would detach himself and slip down a side street. There he would find a quiet spot, usually in a park, take out a book from under his running vest, and settle down to read. There he would remain, with one eye glancing down the road until he saw or heard his mates pass the end of the road. Then he would race after them and reattach himself to the back of the crocodile. It seems hard to believe that the teacher leading them never noticed his absence, but he always got away with it. He did not need the extra exercise, but he certainly benefitted from the extra reading.

Arthur learned how to use his knowledge of science in many ways, one of which was of considerable benefit to his class. The Masters used to rotate between classes at the end of lessons. Sometimes they might walk into their next class to find the room in chaos or a full scale battle taking place, quite a normal event with teenagers. This could result in repercussions which were best avoided.

Arthur solved this by arranging for the previous class to give a warning that the Master was on his way. The classrooms were linked together by iron pipes serving the radiators, and so Arthur solved the problem of providing an advanced warning by getting someone, as soon as the master left the room, to tap the pipe beside him. The tapping would travel along the pipe, far faster than the master could walk, and be emitted from the radiator beside Arthur's seat. This enabled the class to be in perfect control when the master arrived, which must have been a great surprise to many of the teachers. I rather think the science master tumbled to what was happening, but he was very proud of Arthur, and I don't think he decided to mention it.

I also found ways to annoy the masters, but my efforts were rather less subtle. The masters' retiring room was on the first floor of a block which stood between two playgrounds. The masters would sit in front of a huge fire, reading their papers, or correcting the pupils' work. The chimney from this fire stood up well above the roof. I would organize two teams and acquire a tennis ball, preferably belonging to someone else, and they would hurl it from one playground to the other, the object being to drop the ball down the chimney. When this occurred, burning logs and soot covered the masters but by the time they got down to the playgrounds there would be no one there! This was great practice for the Cricket Team, though we rarely won.

Every morning before classes started, the whole school would assemble in the main hall for prayers and a hymn. The pupil who played the piano was a rather delicate young man. One morning as he opened the piano he was engulfed in a most atrocious smell, and had to rush from the room. It was discovered that someone had placed a Kipps apparatus inside the instrument. This piece of apparatus is designed to produce the scent of rotten eggs (which Arthur would have recognised as hydrogen sulphide) for what purpose I could never fathom. However, it was normally locked away in the Chemistry laboratory. How it got taken out no one knew. Although Arthur, who was one of the few people allowed into the lab, was questioned he was never suspected for no one believed he would do a thing like that. Later the suspect was caught, and received a public thrashing from the Headmaster's cane in front of the whole school. The incident was never repeated.

Arthur's brother Michael tends to the horses at Ballifants

Nora with Arthur, Fred, Mary and Michael Clarke

"Gypsies on Cothelstone Hill", the Clarke Family

Grandmother's house, North Hill, Minehead

*Arthur in his study
at Ballifants*

*Charles Wright Clarke, father of
Arthur and Fred Clarke*

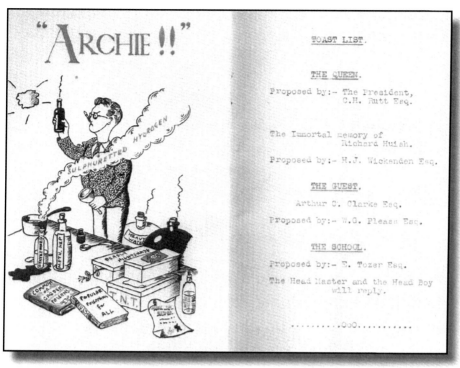

"ARCHIE!!"

TOAST LIST.

THE QUEEN.

Proposed by:- The President,
C.H. Rutt Esq.

The Immortal memory of
Richard Huish.
Proposed by:- H.J. Wickenden Esq.

THE GUEST.

Arthur C. Clarke Esq.
Proposed by:- W.G. Pleass Esq.

THE SCHOOL.

Proposed by:- E. Tozer Esq.

The Head Master and the Head Boy
will reply.

. . . . .OoO. . . . .

Huish Grammar School 1953 Re-union Dinner, depicts Archie (Arthur C. Clarke) getting up to some mischief. Arthur was a guest for this event.

Huish Grammar School

Every young man in those days possessed a catapult, but one lad had to outdo the others. His weapon was the size of a book and had four strings of thick elastic; to match it his ammunition consisted of half-inch diameter ball bearings.

However, the facilities of showing off such a treasure to your friends are rather limited in a school. To overcome this he drew a target on the classroom blackboard. This had one disadvantage: when the ball hit the target it buried itself into the wood, and had to be dug out with a scout knife. That left an incriminating hole, so this was covered up by filling it with well chewed gum mixed with blackening. We thought we'd gotten away with it until one of the Masters, when writing on the board, lost his chalk - it had sunk into the woodwork. The instrument was rapidly discovered and impounded, before being returned to Ballifants.

Arthur was especially interested in science and chemistry. Because of this he had the run of the Chemistry Laboratory, situated in the basement of the school. This was a great help because it solved his lunch problem, and mine. There were no school meals in those days, so we made our own sandwiches and took them to school. Arthur would collect me and we would go down to the basement Labs and wash the sulphuric acid or other noxious fluids from a couple of beakers. Then we would boil some water over the Bunsen Burners, add an *Oxo* cube, and enjoy a hot meal.

Sometimes we forgot to bring the sandwiches, but we could buy a Bun or doughnut from the tuck shop, and this, with hot Oxo, made a unique meal.

On another occasion Arthur was cycling home on the road which runs along the foothills of the Quantock Hills, seeing nothing in front of him further than six foot away. He came to a cross road meeting a steep lane running down from the hills. As he reached the centre he hit another cyclist and at full pelt. They locked together, seats to handlebars. They spun in a complete circle and broke apart. Still facing their original directions they continued straight on, waved to each other, and never met again!

Early Experiments – Wired into the Universe: Asylums, Alien Invasions and Broadcasting to the Solar System

Arthur's favourite uncle was George Grimstone. He was the husband of Father's eldest sister, Zebah, but was also an engineer, being the chief engineer of Cotford Mental Hospital, half a mile away. He encouraged Arthur in his interest in anything mechanical and would send him pieces of engineering and get him to find out what it was and how it worked.

In a large hospital there were always items that required repair so Uncle George would take Arthur to his workshop and together they would repair it. In addition, there were sometimes items that would not be wanted again. Among these were a number of telephone sets, for when the original hospital system was replaced with an automatic one, the old receivers and a lot of wire ended up at Ballifants. George showed Arthur how to connect them up and left Arthur to use the rest. Arthur's first effort was a communications system between his study and the kitchen, so that he could keep in touch and know when food was available. The fact that Mother's voice could carry throughout the house made it rather pointless, but it was a start.

Then Arthur got a little too ambitious. We had a couple of elderly ladies staying at Ballifants and one evening they came rushing out to Mother in great distress. They had been listening to the nine o'clock news on the wireless, when they heard a most frightening announcement. It was a government emergency, warning that the world was being attacked by beings from another planet, and no one should look up into the sky as their eyes would be burnt out by invisible rays!

Mother rushed into the lounge, but on the way she noticed there was a wire trailing from Arthur's study to the room occupied by the two elderly guests. This immediately raised Mother's suspicion. On her way back through the hall she grabbed an item from among the horse saddles that were kept there, ready for the next rider. It was very rare that she used any chastisement, particularly on Arthur, but this was exceptional. Shortly thereafter there was a scream from the wireless, and a sound like a carpet being beaten. Then mother came back in, looking rather dishevelled, and apologised to the guests, explaining that Arthur had been listening to a play and had got his wires crossed with their set. She took them into the kitchen to calm them down with strong coffee, and some stories of her own. Arthur was kept out of the way for several days, in case he was asked how the play ended.

Meanwhile he was working on his next project. He had fixed up two telephone sets in opposite corners of the home field, but a shortage of wire meant a certain amount of improvisation. He traced a pair of wires from the field fence which appeared to be suitable, but the reproduction was awful. The wire had many joins where the animals had forced against it and the twisted knots which re-joined it were an impossible barrier to his worn out acid batteries. However, Arthur had another project in mind. He knew that communications between planets and spaceships would not be able to rely on hundreds of miles of copper wire, so another way would have to be found. And Uncle George found it. When the hospital cinema projector broke down George ordered two spare photoelectric cells for standbys, one of which he arranged to be kept at Ballifants, in Arthur's care. With the help of Mother's powerful farm flashlight, with a telephone mouthpiece wired into the circuit, he found that he could transmit speech through a light beam to the cell. His stories could now spread across the solar system and beyond, and have ever since!

Star gazing - Dunghill Observatory and the Marvels of Meccano

Among the many presents that Arthur was given as a teenager was one of the larger collections of Meccano. At that time he was also working on his short stories about travel to the Moon and he thought he ought to know more about the background for these stories. He already had a telescope, but that needed a stand to hold it, while he was drawing the mountains and plains which covered the Moon's surface. So he collected all the parts of his Meccano set, bought a few extra pieces and gears, and assembled the lot into a magnificent stand. This can be seen in the corner of the picture showing his study at Ballifants.

Arthur took this picture himself by flashlight. After a lot of wasted time and material, trying to get me to set off the flash at the right time, he disposed of my services and organised his own multitalented skills. He hung a piece of magnesium from the ceiling, set a table underneath it and on the table he placed a lighted candle in its holder. To the handle he tied a piece of string and when the scene was set to his liking, he would pull the candle underneath the magnesium. The result was a blinding flash, but more importantly, it arrived when he wanted it. This arrangement worked perfectly until one day Mother came into the room and found a big, black burn just under the bed in the front room. After that, Arthur had to revert to my services, with far less success.

Arthur would go out every evening after doing his homework. His purpose was to get a detailed picture of the edge of the Moon, when the mountains were shown in relief by reflected sunlight. Unfortunately, after sitting for hours in his overheated study, he would rush out into the cold night, with his chair and telescope, without a jacket or pullover. As a result he caught

Arthur and telescope

pneumonia, which was nearly the end of what had promised to be a very profitable career! When he recovered he set out to find a more sheltered spot and found just the place. It stood between a wall and the side of the stables, and had a clear view across the fields and sky. Unfortunately, Mother required the same spot herself and a few days later he found it was occupied by a heap of freshly cleared manure from the stable. However, Arthur persisted, as did Mother, and his line of sight rose a little each day. It was also a rather infirm base on which to set his delicate, steel-framed Meccano telescope stand, the legs of which sank into the foundations at differing rates. This did not improve Arthur's elaborate gearing system, or the value of the set. So Arthur rebuilt a more substantial arrangement out of a smashed-up hen house, which his friend Val Cleaver designated Dunghill Observatory!

Arthur cleaned up and kept his Meccano set, and it was his pride and joy for the rest of his life. When he went to live in Sri Lanka I packed it away in its case and sent it to him. He spent many more years playing with the set, and teaching his young friends how to use it.

The Meccano Set that Fred Sent to Sri Lanka

Arthur with the Meccano Set

The Kille Family and the Bones of an Ammonite

The Kille family lived at the end of Blenheim Road, just three houses away from Arthur's grandmother and Aunt Nellie. They were a lively family and great fun, so Arthur spent a great deal of time with them. Arthur played with the children, had long conversations with the highly educated adults, and there was always food available.

One afternoon, Mrs Kille was not feeling very well, so she told the children to prepare their own tea, and bring her tea into her study, where she fell asleep on the settee. After a while the children did indeed bring Mrs Kille her tea, but the first thing she noticed was that it was laid on her best china. She remonstrated but they said they would be very careful, and the girls sat beside their mother.

Sometime later when she had nearly finished she heard an almighty crash from the kitchen. She rushed to see what had happened but the girls held her back, saying they would make certain everything was all right. They soon returned and told her there was nothing to worry about. However, ten minutes later there was another crash and again the girls said they would attend to it. After another crash and a lot of noise from the kitchen, Mrs Kille rushed out, to find the youngest boy with half a dozen steel plates, strung on a piece of string, which when dropped onto the stone floor made a sound like crashing china!

Arthur learnt a lot from the Kille family which he appreciated all his life. Mr Kille took him along the edge of the Bristol Channel, describing to him the different stones and layers of rock. This started him collecting rocks, which he kept for many years. One such rock that he kept all his life was a piece of stone in which was embedded the fossil of an ammonite.

Adventures with Planes and Rockets – Belated Apologies to Dulborough

One of Arthur's friends was a lad called Dulborough. He lived a couple of miles away from Ballifants in a little village called Halse. He was a clever lad and very skilled, and his great passion was constructing model aeroplanes. These were beautifully intricate creations built from wood, cotton fabric and glue, then lovingly painted. Dulborough's only problem was that there was nowhere available in Halse to test and fly them, so he used to cycle over to Ballifants and test them in the fields there. He always had an audience consisting of myself, Arthur and the rest of the family, who helped to measure how far they flew and to give him advice! Usually about fifty paces was the limit, but when we suggested that he launch them from the roof of Ballifants he was not too keen.

One day, we set his latest masterpiece on top of a gate post, wound the elastic to its limit, and launched it across the field. However, that only added a few feet to its record, until Arthur came up with his master idea. He had been experimenting with gunpowder, grinding the separate constituents - sulphur, charcoal and saltpetre – into powder in his mother's pestle and mortar before mixing them together. He had made this into rockets, which flew very satisfactorily across the field, in fact much further than Dulborough's plane. So Arthur suggested tying one of his rockets to the bottom of Dulborough's plane; this would lift it higher and the plane would go much further.

Dulborough was not happy with the idea, and there was a long argument, which Arthur eventually won. Finally he was allowed to tie his rocket to the magnificent plane, set it on the gatepost and point it to the field away from the house. Dulborough was given the honour of lighting the blue touch paper, an opportunity which he regretted for the rest of his life, and we all stood well away as the combination vehicle shot high into the air. Not very far. As the rocket poured fumes and hot smoke out of the back, the flames licked over the balsa wood and the lacquered plane, and the whole construction fell in a burning tangle fifty paces in front of us.

Dulborough and Arthur rushed to rescue anything that could be salvaged, but there was very little. Dulborough poured what he could into a tin container in his haversack and cycled back to Halse. We did not see him again for quite some time. However, the two boys remained friends, although Dulborough never brought another plane back to Ballifants. Some forty years later both men must have seen the first jet assisted plane take to the air, and later, a great many jets sail across the sky. And Arthur must have thought: That was my idea!

Later Arthur was offered a flight into space but never took it. Like Dulborough, he joined the Royal Air Force, but kept his feet on the ground.

Helping the Fire Brigade

Arthur was always ready to help even when his help was not always required! One afternoon he was passing Quirk Street when he saw the doors of the Fire Station begin to open. He watched the Engine come out, followed by its associated transport.

As the men and materials were being loaded, Arthur offered to help and was finally asked to collect some small items. However, in the course of the loading Arthur somehow found his way into one of the carriages, and ended at a burning cottage at North Hill. How he acquitted himself is not recorded, but he managed to get left behind again. Luckily someone found him and took him back to Blenheim for a very late supper, during which he explained his services to the Fire Brigade.

The Perils of Cycling – Watch out for the Elephant!

As Arthur got older Mother bought him an old Post Office delivery bicycle. This ancient piece of steel saved her six pence a day and greatly improved Arthur's leg muscles. His method of cycling was a little unorthodox. He would hold his head just over the handle bars, as though reading a book. This gave him extra pressure on the pedals, but did not improve his line of sight, as he had to peer over the top of his glasses.

This caused Arthur a little distress late one evening when he was cycling up a steep hill half way home, for he ran into the back of a large black elephant. When Arthur got home and explained why he was late he was treated a little suspiciously. His brother and sister assumed that he had gone round the bend, just as they'd always anticipated. Even his Mother thought she ought to arrange for him to see a doctor. There were plenty available as Ballifants was only a mile away from a Mental Hospital.

However, all was explained at the weekend, when the edition of *The Somerset County Gazette* arrived. Evidently a circus was appearing at Minehead. It had travelled by train to Taunton Station, but the West Somerset Railway did not have a coach big enough to carry an elephant. So the poor animal had to walk the last twenty miles. For safety it was decided that this should be done at night when there would be no traffic on the main road, so they tied a farm lantern on the elephant's tail and off it went with its mahout.

This was how they managed to encounter Arthur, who was late home from school. Cycling through the dark he failed to see the glimmering lantern ahead, and ran into the back of the huge animal. Later he went to see the circus, and apologized to his new friend. Many years later Arthur became patron to a home for orphaned baby elephants in Sri Lanka.

Arthur at the Elephant Orphanage, Sri Lanka

Morning Rituals – Beware the Carbolic!

Mother was always the first person to get up in the morning. She always slept with her bedroom window partly open so the sounds of the cattle wanting to get out of their sheds would awaken her. She would then go down to the kitchen, light the oil stove and put the kettle on. While this was boiling she would then wake Arthur. He would disappear into the bathroom, and very shortly come down for his morning tea.

One morning this was done so quickly that mother asked him if he had washed properly and returned upstairs to wake his sister Mary. When she returned she checked with Arthur that he had washed properly. When he said he had, she asked him if he had used the soap. He confirmed he had, so she wanted to know why the soap was still dry! He said that was because he had dried it on the towel. Mother was not altogether satisfied, because there was no smell of carbolic on his towel. *"I must have used Mary's, then"*. There was a scream from Mary. *"You know I cannot stand carbolic!"* *"It's all right,"* said Mother. *"They are all in the wash. Now get on with your breakfast."*

Keeping Cool - Cattle Cake and Lost Sheep

Ballifants Farm was in a state of minor panic. Some twenty of Nora's sheep had got through the fence and into the field of Farmer Dollings. This had happened several times before, when Nora's sheep had hopelessly intermingled with his prize flock. Mother had been warned by Farmer Dollings that if it happened again, he would take them away and send them to market. That would have broken Mother's heart for she had brought every one of her sheep into this world.

Mother shouted for every member of the family to help separate the two flocks of sheep. Her screams were heard through the adjoining village, and Mary and I were quickly with her. But Arthur's ears did not hear a sound. When I arrived she sent me to look for Arthur, but there was no sign of him. He was not in his study or bedroom, so I searched the usual places where he would hide himself with a book; still there was no sign of him. It was a dreadfully hot afternoon and I searched in every sheltered spot on the farm, but there was no trace of him. Finally, I looked down towards the river which ran along the side of the home field. There were a few bushes which grew on the banks of the river, so I went down to see if Arthur was hiding there. I was in luck; Arthur was not among the bushes but he was in the river. The water was quite shallow but Arthur had dammed it with stones and was lying in the cooling water, with a book perched on a bigger stone, reading away, happily oblivious to the surrounding panic. I soon got him out, with the help of a few clods of soil. And before long he was sheep chasing with the rest of the family.

By this time the farmer's shepherd had arrived with his van and driven off with Nora's sheep, so she rushed back to the house, got out her bicycle and cycled over to the Dollings farm. There she found her sheep intermingled with the far larger Dollings flock. The farmer and his shepherd were in the field as she marched in and told them both that they had some of her sheep. The farmer said that was not the case, they were all his. If she thought any were hers, she must pick them out.

Luckily Mother didn't need to, for half a dozen of the sheep came up to her, and started nuzzling her coat pocket, looking for the cattle cake they knew she always kept there. The farmer drove them off, but a few minutes later they were back again. This happened several times, until the shepherd, foreseeing trouble, said "They 'ain't ours, Boss." "Then take them back," he responded irritably. So the shepherd put the sheep in his van and took them and Mother back to Ballifants. By this time, Arthur was home, wondering why his supper was so late.

Woolworths and Wartime Ballast – How it all Began

Arthur was always short sighted but it never handicapped his writing. While at Huish he was always telling or writing stories about space. What started him writing science fiction was a visit to Woolworths. Their store in Taunton was right opposite the school entrance, so he used to slip into Woolworths during his lunch hour. The attraction was a counter full of American magazines. These were paperback magazines, brought over as ballast during the war. They were all mixed up together: travel stories, women's magazines and household hints. The ones which intrigued Arthur were the tales of space travel. He would comb through the jumbled books to match up a complete story, which he could then buy for two pence. In addition to these stories there was a section devoted to reader's comments on previous tales. Arthur wrote one day to the editor commenting on the faults in one tale. This caused some comments from other readers, one of which suggested that if Arthur thought he could do better, he should try! So Arthur wrote a story which he sent to the magazine and it was instantly published. With that encouragement he continued and kept submitting tales until he left Huish.

Cider Thieves!

When we were younger we used to make our own cider on the farm. It was kept outside in the barn. When no-one was looking I and Arthur would sometimes go out, turn the tap and have ourselves a nice glass of cider. One day when I was out there and thought no-one saw me, I had a drink and then started to head towards the door. But Mother was there and I got a clip around the ear.

Pyjamas and Rifles

One night we were asleep and heard the sound of loud rifle bullets being fired, a .303 rifle I think. Arthur ran outside in his pyjamas to see what it was. It turned out to be one of the local boys just firing off his rifle for fun. We told him to stop and he did. But we were very concerned with Arthur running around outside as he could have been hit by one of those bullets and then we'd have lost all that he went on to achieve.

Flat and Narrow in London

When Arthur first moved to London he had a very small flat. It was one bedroom with just a bed and a wardrobe. It was so small that when we had conferences in there with more than two people Arthur had to hang out the window to make some space.

Marilyn

When Arthur got married, he phoned me and Mother from New York and said *"here is my new wife"*. We were all quite surprised of course and anxious to meet her. When she came over, Marilyn looked as though she had had a good (posh) childhood and wasn't used to roughing it. Mother used to send us boiled eggs in the post, because eggs were scarce in those days. But we all knew that Arthur liked his eggs soft boiled. Anyway, Arthur said that he fancied an egg and Marilyn insisted on making it for him. But she had never boiled an egg before and she re-boiled an egg that had already been boiled. Arthur cracked the shell off and of course he couldn't eat it. Marilyn was quite offended that he didn't like her cooking and she went off to stay with the Les Shepherd family.

Fred Enlists

When World War Two broke out I was working for the post office but one day I saw a sign for the reserve army to join up. So I did. I went back to the post office but the boss wasn't pleased. He said "you know I can undo it just like that," but he never did because he knew I would do it anyway.

Childhood's End

After he left school, Arthur took the Civil Service examination and won a post with the Audit Department in Whitehall. He continued writing until he found he was earning more from his hobby than he was getting from working in a boring London office, so he gave up his job and lived comfortably on his earnings from books and stories for the rest of his life.

In addition to his interest in space, Arthur became involved in underwater swimming, which is the one way to experience weightlessness on Earth. Whilst diving he used to work for hours practising jobs which would have to be done in space, which is why his tales were always authentic, and why they were also later used in training astronauts.

When Arthur resigned from the Civil Service, he enrolled into the Royal Air Force, and that brought an end to his childhood.

Chapter II - Early Days

From Ego to Fame

by Robert Godwin

Arthur C. Clarke's rapid ascension from young enthusiast to world-wide celebrity happened in the two decades between 1934 and 1954. Although his complete life has been documented in Neil McAleer's outstanding biography *Visionary*, I hope the reader might allow room for just a few more details about those formative years.

Although I never met Arthur we corresponded for about ten years and he was incredibly generous to me. I feel a special kinship with him. Let me briefly explain why.

His favourite place to go as a child was the beach at Minehead where he would play in the tidal pools and watch the wild weather come pounding in from the Atlantic. I grew up in direct sight of that very beach, just 13 miles away on the opposite side of the Bristol Channel. The town where I lived was like a mirror image of Minehead with its narrow streets, whitewashed houses, tiny fishing harbour and concrete seawall; which held back one of the largest tidal ranges in the world. The ocean front road even had the same name - *Esplanade*. Just as Arthur did, I would ride my bike to the beach after school (800 yards for me, only 300 for Arthur,) play in the tidal pools, collect fossils, and then dodge the giant waves on the seawall when the tide came in, which it oftentimes did with a vengeance, carried on the back of the powerful Westerlies. On a tough winter day the waves would throw fish onto the porches of the seafront homes and then when the tide receded it would expose a clear mile of sand to the sky. From a very early age I knew the danger of being caught too far out on that sand at the wrong time of day and I developed a healthy respect for the ocean.

In 2004 when the pictures of the Indian Ocean tsunami appeared on my television it was a replay of my worst childhood nightmares and when I heard it might hit Sri Lanka my first thought was for Arthur. But, if he knew what I knew about the infamous *Severn Bore*, which surfers could ride on a good day and my grandmother used to use as a sort of boogieman to keep me safe, I knew he would be safely away from the beach. Although I had shared the same weather, the same geology, same sunsets, same tides, same smells of seaweed, ozone and salt and I occasionally used to take the ferry over to Lundy Island on Arthur's side, I was thirty-five years too late to meet that bespectacled young man who dreamed of a cosmic ocean. But there was something powerfully elemental about that part of planet Earth which is permanently ingrained in me and maybe in some small way it explains why I was so drawn to Arthur's exceptional writing from as early as I can remember.

When we accept that someone is exceptional it is typically due to some evidence of original thought or natural inventiveness. Exceptional people usually have the courage of their convictions and they often exude confidence; or sometimes it is just sheer hard work that makes them stand out. Then there are the people who are all of these things and they seem to explode into history fully-formed. Arthur C. Clarke was just such a person and, although he was clearly inspired, there is no evidence that he ever had a mentor. At the age of seven years old Clarke was delivering rudimentary science lectures to his classmates. Then during one twelve-month period between 1930 and 1931 he encountered two books which he claimed changed his life. David Lasser's *The Conquest of Space* and Olaf Stapledon's *Last and First Men*. The former he encountered in the window of a book shop and the latter in the Minehead library. Lasser opened his eyes to the imminent probability of spaceflight and Stapledon's mainly pantheistic themes guided Clarke's fiction for the rest of his life. However, both Lasser and Stapledon were too far removed to play mentor to Clarke. Although, perhaps tellingly, both of them also grew up next to the ocean in port towns.

Clarke's first writings appeared between 1932 and 1936 in the Huish Grammar school magazine. More than two dozen short pieces appeared under a variety of pseudonyms, including "Ego," the less than flattering nickname that he would wear like a badge of honour for the rest of his life. As Fred Clarke has already related, Arthur's childhood ended when he left Somerset for London.

Although he still didn't find a mentor in London, he certainly would find many kindred spirits. They would come into his life through an assortment of clubs, societies and associations; the most important of these was *The British Interplanetary Society* which he had joined through correspondence while still at Huish. The story of Arthur Clarke's interactions with his friends in the 1930s and 40s requires a complex tour of these clubs, but at the core of the story is a young man who had access to a multitude of amateur publications where he could hone his penmanship and refine his original concepts and stories.

London, Leeds, Leicester and Liverpool — four of England's largest industrial cities – were jokingly referred to as the four "Hells". In the early 19th century the Leeds-Liverpool canal was the main artery running through the beating heart of the industrial revolution—the city of Manchester. Another canal connected the textile industry in Manchester to the old Roman fort town of Leicester. For generations every form of transportation known to man had been used by travellers commuting between these cities, but in the 1930s the railway allowed a small group of ambitious young men to stay in constant contact while they planned the next step in human transportation. These young idealists gave birth to an assortment of amateur societies and clubs between 1933 and the beginning of World War II. They included The British Interplanetary Society, *The Leeds Rocket Society*, *The Manchester Interplanetary Society*, *The Astronautical Development Society*, *The Science Fiction Association* and *The Combined British Astronautical Societies*. For over a decade this small group of young men organized and planned meetings and rode the rails from one end of the country to the other to discuss a future that they knew would inevitably involve humans voyaging into space. Even World War II barely slowed them down. There may not have been a mentor at the heart of this band of dreamers but there was certainly a catalyst.

Philip Cleator, the sprightly founder of the British Interplanetary Society (BIS), was the godfather of British astronautics. Cleator came from the exact same seaside town where Olaf Stapledon had been born. Perched on the end of the Wirral peninsula the small town of Wallasey overlooked the Mersey river where a young man could watch the comings and goings of the world through the giant port of Liverpool. For a hundred years Liverpool stood as perhaps the most important transportation and commercial hub in the world. It seems that for young men like Cleator and Stapledon (and Lasser, who grew up in Baltimore, another major port) it also inspired ambitious dreams of the future. Similarly Clarke would have watched the wealth of ocean vessels trafficking in and out of Bristol and Cardiff. Seeing the ocean horizon near a large port is a strong incentive to develop a broader perspective on life and Clarke would ultimately never foresake the ocean.

From his home in the Wirral Cleator fought a solitary battle for three years against ridicule and indifference; struggling to have the new science of astronautics taken seriously in England; then in late 1933 he decided to establish a formal society to promote spaceflight and things very slowly started to improve. About ten months after launching his tiny group of space advocates a sixteen-year-old boy, living on a small farm in England's West Country, applied for membership. His name, of course, was Arthur Charles Clarke and more than any of his contemporaries he would become the unchallenged champion of space flight, rocketry and astronautics in Britain for many years to come.

As the BIS expanded Cleator and many of the other very early British pioneers would gradually fade into the sunset, some of them would be lost in the war; but Clarke would campaign tirelessly from the moment he joined the Society. He became club secretary, then treasurer, then chairman; he edited and wrote large chunks of the club Bulletin, he wrote to the newspapers, he gave public addresses, he wrote space fiction and he provided encouragement to every single mimeographed publication that so much as *mentioned* space (and also wrote for many of them.) After the war ended, working from his elevated position as BIS Chairman, he finally had a forum where his ideas could begin to alter the world. There can be little doubt that Cleator's BIS provided the catalyst that led Clarke away from his family's pastoral existence and out into a wider universe where he would encounter a precocious group of like-minded individuals.

One of those individuals was Maurice Hanson; science fiction fan, BIS member, mathematician and aspiring publisher and editor. Hanson's catalyst was not Cleator, but American science fiction pioneer Hugo Gernsback who issued a rallying call to fans around the world to establish local branches of his correspondence club named the *Science Fiction League*. Hanson immediately responded by establishing the 22nd chapter in his home town of Nuneaton. Like others before him he then began his own fan magazine; he called it *Novae Terrae*. Hanson had joined the BIS in February 1936 and he published the first issue of Novae Terrae a month later.

Despite its primitive mimeographed format it soon attracted many of the alumni of the young British Interplanetary Society, including Clarke who had been reading Gernsback's magazines since the 1920s.

Novae Terrae was just one of a flood of amateur publications generated in England between 1935 and 1945 which included *The Fantast, Futurian War Digest, Satellite, Urania, Zenith, Tomorrow, The Astronaut, Amateur Science Stories, Spacewards* and *Fan Mail*. Then there were the more professionally produced *Tales of Wonder, New Worlds* and the *Journal of the British Interplanetary Society* (JBIS). The one thing these all had in common was Arthur C. Clarke.

As much a forum for short fiction as a place to vent opinion, Novae Terrae would last for three years and twenty-nine issues. For all of its brief tenure and amateur appearance, Novae Terrae provides useful insights into the minds of the group of aspiring rocketeers who surrounded Clarke in his late teens and early 20s. There are some truly hilarious articles (some of which are included in this book) that reveal the wit and fun surrounding this small group of friends who went on to forge the British Interplanetary Society into one of the world's most respected Space organisations.

In the 1930s space flight was generally considered to be pure fantasy by both the man in the street and the scientific community; but Clarke already knew better. He joined the BIS in the late summer of 1934 and by November of 1936 he had risen to society treasurer. He loved his science fiction as much as his science fact and over the next few years he would become an important player in both worlds. Straddling the fence, he would bring clarity to fact and sanity to fiction.

Clarke's initiation into the world of the SFL began with a journey north to one of the four "Hells", the Yorkshire town of Leeds. It was there that Clarke met up with Douglas Mayer, another aspiring publisher and writer.

Mayer and his school friends had formed a Leeds chapter of Gernsback's Science Fiction League back in 1935 and almost every day they would spend time surrounded by books and magazines at the group's clubroom. At these impromptu gatherings they would discuss rocketry and the latest stories appearing in the American pulps. At that time Clarke was unaware of this group but he wrote a letter to *Amazing Stories* which appeared in the February 1935 issue asking to be put into contact with other British science fiction readers. This letter would be the first piece of Clarke writing to appear in America.

The Leeds group would play a major role in Clarke's involvement with the fledgling British science fiction movement. Mayer's diaries still survive, one of which begins on December 10th 1936, the day of the abdication of King Edward VIII. It reveals that all through December and January Mayer had meetings with his colleagues about a national conference they were planning for science fiction and spaceflight fans. On December 10th he indicates that they were about to form a "rocket section" of their club; this may have been at the instigation of another member named Harold Gottliffe; although this isn't entirely made clear in Mayer's diary. On the 13th Mayer proposed to the other members a "British non-commercial organization" which would be formed by merging the various SFL chapters into one national club. At this point the group had been discussing their proposed science fiction conference since at least October of 1936. Mayer advertised it in the November and December 1936 issues of Hanson's Novae Terrae and told people that they had to arrange for their tickets in advance. He listed a group of names who had agreed to attend, a meeting hall was rented, speakers were arranged and advance sales of a program were organized. Mayer's diary also makes it clear that for this group there was little distinction between the science fiction and rocketry community. Before the event Mayer compiled a file of research on rocketry, and the group spent time designing a proving stand and a "petrol-air" rocket; which they later considered launching for publicity purposes, although it seems clear that it was never built. On December 15th the group even conducted an interview with the Leeds Mercury newspaper about rocketry. This subset of Clarke's friends would become known briefly as the *Leeds Rocket Society*.

In the small hours of January 3rd 1937 newly appointed BIS Secretary/ Treasurer Arthur C. Clarke and Chairman Edward John (Ted) Carnell caught the mail train from St Pancras to Leeds to attend the event, which was now named the *First British Science Fiction Conference* and was to be held at the Theosophical Hall in Leeds. Their friend Walter Gillings, another BIS member and soon to be the publisher of Britain's first professionally produced science fiction magazine, travelled along with them. Maurice Hanson joined the train en route in Leicester. Two of Mayer's colleagues, George Airey and Albert Griffiths diligently waited at the railway station all night to greet the London entourage.

A composite photograph of the "London Entourage" outside the Leeds Theosophical Hall. Left to right, Walter Gillings, Arthur C. Clarke, Ted Carnell and Maurice Hanson. (From two images taken moments apart by Harold Gottliffe, courtesy Jill Godfrey.)

As fate would have it, this gathering turned out to be the first real science fiction convention held anywhere in the world. Fourteen people showed up from the four "Hells" and at least six of them were members of the British Interplanetary Society; including Les Johnson, who had been secretary of the BIS since its inception, and science fiction author Eric Frank Russell, who both arrived late in the day from Liverpool.

At the Leeds convention the various regional groups of the League combined to officially form the *Science Fiction Association* and Clarke joined along with everyone else. His membership in this newly formed national group would ultimately bring Clarke to the attention of almost all of the organized groups of science fiction fans in England and provide an outlet for most of his early writings. One of these outlets would be *British Scientifiction Fantasy Review* a fanzine which Walter Gillings announced at the conference. Clarke delivered a short speech to the Leeds attendees notifying everyone that the BIS had now opened a new branch in London. This new London offshoot had been established because there were more people in London to draw upon for potential members than in Liverpool where the Society had been based. By the time Clarke and Carnell had arrived in Leeds the decision had already been made to move the entire management of the BIS to London.

The resolution to move BIS HQ from Liverpool to London would propel Clarke into a much more active role than had been previously possible. One of the decisions that had been made at the first London meeting, back on October 27th 1936, was that Clarke would replace Les Johnson as secretary and that Carnell would be the new chairman. Less than three weeks later Johnson came down from Liverpool and at that meeting Clarke would also be elected Honorary Treasurer.

The Leeds conference was enough of a success to begin a trend of annual British science fiction conventions which continue almost uninterrupted to this very day. In a rare moment of good fortune Harold Gottliffe decided to bring along his camera and record the day for posterity. The images show a wiry-thin 19-year-old Clarke standing with his friends in the street outside the terraced front of the Theosophical hall.

Eleven of the fourteen attendees of the world's first science fiction convention; Leeds January 3rd 1937. Left to right, Maurice K. Hanson, Arthur C. Clarke, Walter H. Gillings, Leslie J. Johnson, Edward J. Carnell, Eric Frank Russell, Herbert Warnes, George A. Airey, Alec Miller, Douglas W.F. Mayer, J. Michael Rosenblum. This group would collectively be responsible for at least nine different astronautical and science fiction publications. (Photograph by Harold Gottliffe, courtesy Jill Godfrey)

On January 20th Mayer mailed copies of his pre-arranged summary of the convention to the club members. The following month he became the first of the Leeds convention attendees to write an article for the Journal of the British Interplanetary Society. His critique of H.G. Wells' *Things to Come* (later stated to be Clarke's favourite movie) would appear just below the official announcement that the BIS was moving not only the headquarters from Liverpool to London but that the Journal of the BIS would follow suit. Six months later Carnell began editing the next issue of JBIS from London in what would be the first in a string of journals continuing almost uninterrupted for the next eight decades.

However, from February 1937 until early 1938 the Journal of the BIS was unavoidably delayed due to the overhaul of the society's structure. The issue originally slated for December didn't appear until February 1938. Consequently for about a year Novae Terrae and the *Bulletin of the British Interplanetary Society* became the principal places where the members could communicate official business outside of their monthly meetings.

In June, at the age of just nineteen years old Clarke submitted an essay to Hanson for inclusion in Novae Terrae; entitled *Science Fiction Past Present and Future* (see below.) His assertions in this short article have become today's paradigms in the world of science fiction. But in 1937, these were highly original and extremely well conceived notions, blossoming forth from a teenager destined for greatness. Clarke would become Hanson's associate editor just four months later and it is not difficult to understand why his friend thought he was well-suited to that position. Not only would Clarke co-edit Novae Terrae but in the year before the war he would almost single-handedly edit the Bulletin of the BIS.

True to his word Walter Gillings started publishing his British Scientifiction Fantasy Review almost immediately after the Leeds convention. This would be Gilling's first serious publication and he found Clarke and Mayer were willing confederates and supported his plan for a well-produced fanzine for shedding light on the latest books and science fiction stories. In October Clarke submitted his review to Gillings of the novel *Zero to Eighty* by Akkad

Pseudoman. Not surprisingly *Mr Pseudoman* was a thin attempt to disguise the identity of the real author Ernest Northrup, a Princeton physicist. Clarke's review of the book was generally a positive one since he recognised the hand of a scientist at work in the text. Northrup had in fact been the earliest researcher to work on what at the time was known as "long pull magnets". Northrup's story postulated the use of a rail gun for launching a payload into space, a concept still under discussion today. The gun is 200km long and financed by a gold mine discovery. Clarke wrote, *"Here the author strains our imagination rather severely for it is unlikely the most fabulous gold mine could provide for such a monster which makes Wells' Space Gun look like a pea shooter."* In later years Clarke would never dismiss an idea as long as it didn't defy the laws of physics, even if it might seem over-zealous to the average onlooker; a fact evidenced by his support of the Space Elevator which would make even Northrup's rail gun pale by comparison. More than a dozen years later Clarke would take the rail gun concept to new heights in both his fiction and a paper he would write for the BIS.

Meanwhile, back in Leeds, Douglas Mayer, who by now had two issues in print of his own science and science fiction magazine called *Tomorrow*, decided to try another publishing experiment. In the summer 1937 issue of Tomorrow Mayer announced,*"...as a three months' experiment, the publication of three issues of AMATEUR SCIENCE STORIES. Each issue will contain one or more science-fiction stories by amateur authors. All stories received for consideration will be passed on to a committee (to be appointed later) who will award marks -- some marks for originality, some marks for development of plot, some marks for style, etc. Stories receiving more than a certain total of marks will be accepted and published... Should the experiment prove of interest, the magazine will be continued indefinitely."*

Amateur Science Stories only appeared for the three preordained issues, because Mayer said it didn't attract enough contributors. Those three issues arrived in October and December 1937 and March 1938. Almost half of the content published by Mayer came from Clarke. The December issue featured his *Travel by Wire* which was a two page comedy about a matter transmitter being used for, amongst other things, weight loss. The March issue featured

How We Went to Mars, a parody of a manned Mars trip made by a rocket society; followed by *Retreat from Earth*, a highly improbable story of a termite colony with a super-computer as a central brain defending Earth from invading Martians. Amateur Science Stories gives Douglas Mayer the distinction of being the first person to ever publish Clarke's fiction to a paying audience at sixpence a copy, or 35 cents to readers in the USA. Mayer had the presence of mind to actually sell bound copies of all three issues for the discounted price of a shilling a copy. (There are a few fans out there that might pay a little more for one of those today!)

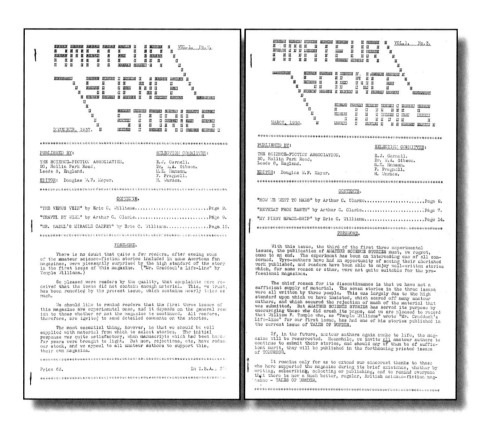

Issues #2 and #3 of Douglas Mayer's Amateur Science Stories where the fiction of Arthur C. Clarke made its first major appearance.
(Courtesy: Kevin Mayer)

Douglas William Frank Mayer, organiser of the world's first science fiction convention and the first publisher of fiction by Arthur C. Clarke. (Courtesy: Kevin Mayer)

During the summer of 1937, despite its meagre finances, the BIS "Technical Committee" began serious research into a spacecraft capable of reaching the moon. Clarke, ostensibly appointed as the group's astronomer, delivered talks about the moon during a meeting on May 4th. BIS member William F. Temple later recollected in his diary that astronomy seemed to be yet another one of Clarke's fortés, *"Gillings, myself, Smith, Edwards, Clarke and Janser strolled along to Oxford circus...Clarke held me in discussion on books of astronomy."*

The initial report of the technical committee's work on the lunar spacecraft first appeared in the delayed issue of JBIS in February 1938. Around the same time Clarke wrote another piece for Gillings' fanzine entitled *Science Fiction for the Beginner*. Later that year Gillings began his professionally produced magazine *Tales of Wonder* which featured a lengthy essay by Clarke taking the reader on a tour of the solar system. At this time it was still believed that Venus was a primitive water and jungle world but Clarke was amongst the sceptics when it came to Martian canals and his knowledge of planetary astronomy was in clear evidence in this long article.

1938 would be a particularly fertile year for the young Arthur Clarke. He had previously joined a group in Glasgow called the *Junior Astronomical Association*. In October of 1937 he had written a rebuttal to an article called *"The Case Against Space Travel"* which had appeared in the association's journal *Urania*. In this two page essay he addressed all of the principal objections to spaceflight; providing explanations of passive thermal control, artificial gravity, cosmic ray protection, atmospheric control and fuel/weight ratios. He also explained the mathematics of Tsiolkovsky's famous spaceflight equation. This seems to have spurred him into action to head off any further misinformation reaching the readers of Urania because, starting in April 1938, a formal Astronautical Section was formed which included Clarke and Eric Burgess of the *Manchester Astronautical Society*. The two then began a long-running series of articles called "*An Outline of Astronautics*". This series would include the following essays by Clarke: 1. *Obstacles*, 2. *The Rocket Motor*, 3. *Power*, 4. *The Space Ships*, 5. *The Path of the Space Ship*, 6. *More Orbits*, 7. *Some Fuels*, and 8. *Dangers*. Clarke would make some forgivable errors, (he thought a lunar vehicle would only cost £1,000,000) but for the most part it was a clear overview of the science of astronautics as it was understood at that time.

In the Spring of 1938 Clarke would write a letter to *Astounding Science Fiction* magazine in the USA in response to yet another ill-informed article about space flight. He carefully explained the mathematics of Tsiolkovsky's famous spaceflight equation (again) and obviously made an impression on the editor because the letter appeared in its entirety. That editor was none other than the notorious John Campbell, making Clarke's letter one of the first editorial choices made by Campbell, who had taken over the full editorship of Astounding with the issue that featured the letter. It had been over three years since his letter to Amazing Stories and only the second appearance in print for Clarke in America. Coincidentally about three weeks later Campbell first met Isaac Asimov who along with Clarke and another Campbell discovery, Robert Heinlein, would later comprise the "Big Three" writers of the Golden Age of science fiction.

On July 17th US Navy Midshipman and rocket pioneer Robert Truax arrived in England to speak to the BIS membership. Truax delivered all of the latest news from the *American Rocket Society,* an organisation that, unlike the BIS, had the resources to actually build experimental rockets. It was left to Clarke to convert and interpret the minutes from that gathering into an article in the August issue of the BIS Bulletin. Photographs taken during Truax' visit have since become iconic images of the BIS during those pre-war years. Clarke also announced in the same Bulletin the affiliation of the BIS with Burgess' Manchester Astronautical Society. Both Burgess and Novae Terrae cover artist Harry Turner had come down from Manchester to meet Truax.

The meeting with Robert Truax on July 17th 1938. Left to right, Harold E. Ross, John Happian Edwards, Eric Burgess, Harold E. Turner, Ralph A. Smith, Robert C. Truax (visiting from America), Maurice K. Hanson and Arthur C. Clarke.

Earlier that year, Clarke, who had been living in a tiny flat not much larger than a closet, in Norfolk Square, London, was visited by William Temple, who was at this point the BIS publicist. Temple took this opportunity to produce what must surely be the first biography of Clarke (see below). Despite his hilarious portrayal of the infamous "Ego", Clarke apparently recognised Temple as a kindred spirit and a month later the duo would take over a flat together about four miles east from "Clarke's Closet," at 88 Grays Inn Road in central London. In November, Novae Terrae editor Hanson would also move into the flat with them. Their home would become a frequent watering hole, mailing address, and general gathering place for the blossoming British Interplanetary Society. All through the rest of 1938 and into 1939 Novae Terrae and the BIS Bulletin would be churned out of the flat; alternately bouncing back and forth between fact and fiction. Events at the three friends' "digs" at 88 Grays Inn Road would later be immortalized in Temple's book of the same name.

In April 1938 Temple wrote in his diary, *"I think the happiest moments*

of my life now are when in the company of my SFA friends – Arthur Clarke,
Maurice, Eric, Sid. How I value such friends! I hate to think that one day we
may have to split up and part. Could we weather the coming war?"

Despite the foreboding final sentiment in Temple's diary entry, his Novae
Terrae biography of Clarke is dripping with wry humour and barely disguises the
competitive nature of their friendship, which is revealed even more in Clarke's
rebuttal salvo seven months later (see below.) Clarkes' biography of Temple
would be the very last article to appear in the last issue, of Novae Terrae.

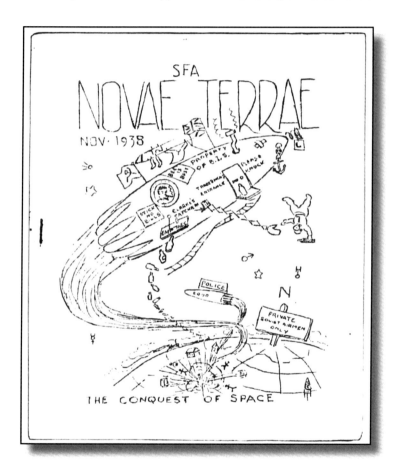

The November 1938 issue of Novae Terrae featured cover art co-designed
by Clarke and Harry Turner (yet another of the early BIS pioneers) and included
the "Clarke Catch'em", a grappling arm which seems to be trying to save a Frank
Poole look-alike from drifting off into space. (Courtesy: Philip Turner)

Finally, in 1939 JBIS would return with a vengeance. The January issue, edited by Temple, included not only the first serious outline for a lunar spacecraft, but also Clarke's first official contribution to the journal, *An Elementary Mathematical Approach to Astronautics*. Clarke had served on the design committee for the BIS spacecraft as the astronomer but it didn't stop him from also branching out into Maurice Hanson's appointed territory as the group's mathematician. With the hindsight of seven decades their design might seem naïve, but it was technically sound, and it was the first time that a group of serious-minded individuals, with an appropriate array of skill sets, had given meaningful thought to all aspects of a lunar spacecraft. All the more remarkable since the entire research fund at the time amounted to £28 12s 0d. Ten pounds of that sum had come from one solitary benefactor.

Clarke had given the BIS membership a "heads-up" on the progress of the Technical Committee in the December 1938 issue of the Bulletin. Referring to the imminent reappearance of JBIS he wrote, "*This Journal is important as marking the end of one stage in the Society's development. It contains, in an exceedingly condensed form, the results of two years of work by the Technical Committee, culminating in the designs of the first practicable space-ship. This ship, we know, could be built in a few years by any competent engineering firm. Our aim now is to conduct such further research work as we can with our slender resources, at the same time doing everything in our power to bring these facts to the notice of the general public and the world of science.*"

He went on to describe how the committee had chosen to spend their time and effort on designing four things; a new battery, a speedometer, an altimeter and a coelostat, rather than building a rocket. This was partly due to the fact that in 1937 His Majesty's government had already invoked an ancient explosives law prohibiting the firing of rockets in England, after Eric Burgess and his team in Manchester had inadvertently injured a spectator when their rocket exploded on the launch pad. Despite this ban Clarke still wrote, "*Many of you have thought this programme a long way from rocket research, but after all, this is not a rocket society. Although we could have shot a number of entertaining rockets with the money at our disposal, it was still far too little to enable us to do any really significant work that had not already been done elsewhere.*"

Clarke was true to his word about promotion being the next step in their plans. Newnes *Practical Mechanics* magazine would feature the BIS design prominently on the cover of its March 1939 issue, a particularly rewarding accolade for the group, since Newnes had also been publisher for H.G. Wells, their spiritual mentor. Writing in his diary Bill Temple would state, *"(I am) editor of the BIS Journal – I have edited the last two, and made something of a publicity splash in the papers with them, though Arthur Clarke has perhaps (almost certainly) done most of the work."*

Somewhat ironically while JBIS featured their plans for using rockets to reach the moon, the newspapers were reporting that they could just as easily be used to bombard cities.

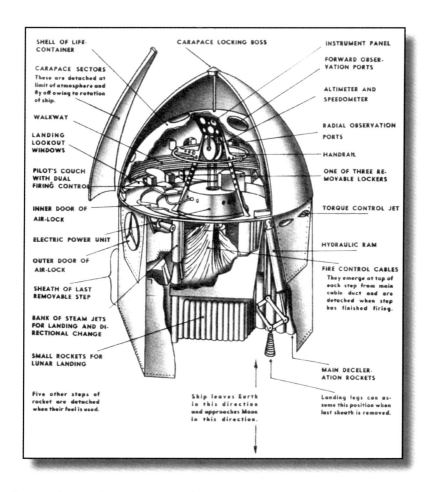

The British Interplanetary Society lunar spacecraft circa 1938. (Courtesy BIS)

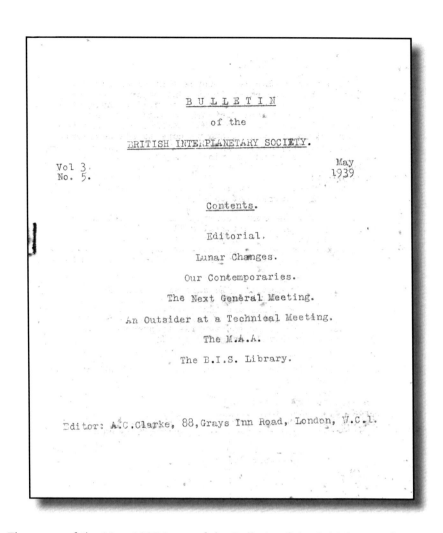

B U L L E T I N

of the

BRITISH INTERPLANETARY SOCIETY.

Vol 3.
No. 5.

May
1939

Contents.

Editorial.

Lunar Changes.

Our Contemporaries.

The Next General Meeting.

An Outsider at a Technical Meeting.

The M.A.A.

The B.I.S. Library.

Editor: A.C.Clarke, 88,Grays Inn Road, London, W.C.1.

The cover of the May 1939 issue of the Bulletin of the British Interplanetary Society. (Courtesy: BIS via Joe Patrizio)

The lunar spacecraft design brought unprecedented attention to the BIS. It was discussed on the radio; in several major journals and in the mainstream newspapers. Clarke led the charge to deflate any contrary opinions which might detract from their carefully constructed paper. Three years earlier McMillans' *Nature* magazine had staked their ground on this issue when the Astronomer Royal had reviewed Cleator's book *Rockets Through Space* and concluded that *"we are forced to dismiss the notion as essentially unpractical."* In the April edition of Nature the editors dismissed the whole idea again with, *"... little confidence can be placed in the deliberations of the British Interplanetary*

Society." Clarke immediately volleyed back with a letter which McMillan chose not to publish, so Clarke published it himself in the BIS Bulletin in May, "*...a serious study should be treated in the scientific spirit,*" he concluded. Despite a decade of evidence to the contrary Clarke was still fighting the same battles that Robert Goddard had fought almost a generation earlier. This encounter with the reviewer in Nature would sew the seed for the first of three laws which Clarke would postulate many years later. Clarke's first law stated: "*When a distinguished but elderly scientist states that something is possible, he is almost certainly right. When he states that something is impossible, he is very probably wrong.*"

At this time the Bulletin of the BIS was virtually Clarke's own personal vehicle for spreading his message. It was being mimeographed at his Gray's Inn flat and it was usually about twelve pages of reports and news; stating clearly on the cover "*Editor: A.C. Clarke*". However, there would always be room for Bill Temple's humour. He wrote an entertaining essay in the May issue describing what it was like to be in the company of some of the members of the BIS Technical Committee; the first group of scientists and engineers to design a lunar space vehicle. Ralph Smith (artist, turbine engineer), John Happian Edwards (director), Arthur Janser (chemist), Clarke (astronomer) and Temple were all in attendance that night. Over the course of the evening the group discussed everything from Smith's latest painting of the Earth as seen from space, to supersonic aircraft design.

In the same issue of the Bulletin Clarke notified the members that the next meeting of BIS would be held at the Royal Aeronautical Society headquarters and that the Bulletin would now be combined with Eric Burgess' competing Manchester Astronautical Society newsletter to avoid repetition of work. In another somewhat snippety aside Clarke reported, "*We read in the Sunday Express that Sir Ambrose Fleming the famous physicist was the man who finally showed that interplanetary travel was impossible. It is a great pity that this information has come so late in the day, had they known it a few years ago it would have saved the Technical Committee so much trouble.*"

Despite all of these "knowledgeable" detractors, Clarke was not to be deterred. The mathematics and chemistry were incontrovertible, and so to Clarke, it was just an engineering problem waiting to be solved; a point that he made eloquently in his rebuttal to Nature's editors. The BIS Bulletin would not be published during the war but it would be revived in January 1946 for a short 18-month run before being permanently discontinued in favour of the full Journal.

Novae Terrae had also run its course by this time, but not before reporting several more amusing anecdotes of Clarke's attempts to indoctrinate his pals with music and movies. His roommate Bill Temple would often do the same with his favourite Douglas Fairbanks swashbucklers. The overall response to these spontaneous movie nights was similar to that clearly described by Michael Moorcock in his anecdotal story from the 1950s (which follows herein.) Moorcock would later be hand-picked by Carnell to take over editorship of the post-war version of Novae Terrae now renamed *New Worlds*.

Despite the superficial grumbling, apparently much fun was had by all at these gatherings, and Clarke was never to be deterred from showing his movies, playing records, singing the odd song or even tormenting his friends with space poetry. One report after a typical meeting reads, *"Hot on his heels came BIS stalwart Arthur C. Clarke to give a recital of s-f gramophone records. Assisted by his famous Ego he gave an admirable rendering of Things to Come and Isle of the Dead."* Later it continues, *"Then melody rang forth again when Arthur Clarke continued with the second part of his recital."*

Clarke's co-editor Ted Carnell would attempt to re-launch Novae Terrae as a slightly-more professionally printed magazine in March 1939, with a new title and with evocative cover art of a spaceship flying through space. Clarke would step in as associate editor in time for the second issue in April 1939 and Temple would return to the fold by the third issue. Despite a valiant effort the team of Clarke, Temple, Hanson and Carnell would only produce four issues of New Worlds, before the whole venture collapsed due to the Nazi invasion of Poland.

In the final pre-war issue of New Worlds Clarke would submit another short piece entitled *Reverie*. This two page essay would take to task those critics who maintained that all of the good science fiction stories had already been written! *"Notwithstanding the pessimists, there are a million million themes that science-fiction has never touched,"* he wrote. Undoubtedly his young imagination was already bursting with notions of strange parallel universes when he continued, *"As long as science advances, as long as mathematics discovers incredible worlds where twice two would never dream of equalling four, so, new ideas will come tumbling into the mind of anyone who will let his thoughts wander, passport in hand, along the borders of Possibility."* And could he actually have been foreseeing the cell phone when he wrote this? *"How odd it would be if someone to whom you were talking via the phone walked into the room and began a conversation with a colleague!"*

Just a few days after this was printed, England would be thrust into conflict with Germany. Once again, in an ironic twist, the newspapers reported that Nazi scientists were working on a rocket to travel to the moon.

In November, with the war now in full swing, BIS meetings continued in London. The group still discussed the idea of keeping New Worlds alive, but circumstances would soon conspire to foil their plans.

Temple recalled in his diary that Clarke was invited to give a lecture to the Archimedeans of Cambridge on 29th November. Today, this group is one of the most prestigious organisations at Cambridge University, but they had only been around for four years when 22-year-old Arthur Clarke arrived to tell them all about space flight. In the same month he returned to the pages of Urania with an essay entitled *Astronomy and Astronautics*. It seems that during a meeting in London some astronomers had voiced the opinion that the science of astronautics was a waste of time. Clarke took them to task and explained how spaceflight would revolutionise astronomy. *"There is not a single aspect of the science – of every science – which will not be immeasurably enriched by the crossing of space,"* he wrote.

The last meeting of the BIS would be held on January 16th 1940. They had abandoned 88 Grays Inn Road on December 29th and so they held the last meeting at Arthur Janser's house. They continued to gather for Science Fiction Association meetings at the Red Bull pub next door to Clarke's Grays Inn flat until May, before circumstances forced the group to finally fragment. Temple was called to service and sent to North Africa and Italy. Hanson was sent to France and Carnell to Algiers. The Red Bull pub was completely flattened by the blitz and Temple later noted that their flat had been damaged in the same raid.

Meanwhile, Clarke who in 1940 had been working as a civil servant, found himself being relocated to the beach front at Colwyn Bay in North Wales; away from the bombing. Colwyn Bay was the location of one of only two Marconi wireless training schools in Britain. Later known as the *Wireless College* it had been there since the 1920s. When war broke out it became one of the most important places in the world for training people to use first radio and later radar. It seems entirely coincidental that Clarke's home was just one street away from the college where he couldn't have missed seeing the giant transmitting mast every morning. Clarke would become heavily involved with the Marconi Company in the years ahead for reasons which have since become obvious. Colwyn Bay was also only a few kilometres from where Stapledon had first found his inspiration to write *Last and First Men*.

While in Wales Clarke began publishing his own newsletter, which due to the paper shortage, literally started out with only five copies of each issue. It was called *Fan Mail* because Clarke decided that the logical way to beat the paper shortage was to print only five copies and then have them *fan* out from one reader to the next. Each reader would then add something to the bottom of the last page and send it on to the next reader. Ultimately the whole thing would then end up back on Clarke's doorstep and he would summarise it all in the next letter. Fan Mail became popular for a while and expanded to 21 readers; comprised predominantly of his London friends. This "analog blog" was announced in one of the few fanzines that continued to operate during the war, *Futurian War Digest* published in Leeds by J. Michael Rosenblum, another of the original fourteen attendees of the first science fiction convention.

Now firmly ensconced on the remote Welsh seaside Clarke decided that rather than waiting to be conscripted it might be best that he volunteer for the service of his choice; somewhere that his skills might be put to good use. He therefore chose to enlist with the RAF and was called up in March 1941; he soon found himself working in the Wiltshire countryside on "Radio Direction Finding", a barely disguised name for the top secret early development of radar. Novae Terrae artist Harry Turner would join him there. Turner would later recall that Clarke continued to give frequent talks to the other recruits about space flight. *"There were arguments raging all over the camp for weeks after the event, with 'Spaceship' Clarke being regarded as either a genius or a complete nut-case!"* Their old friend Douglas Mayer would also be brought into the secret world of radar, but as a civilian scientist after he had indiscreetly suggested in a newspaper article that an atomic weapon might be inevitable. Someone decided he would be of more use working on advanced technology rather than down a coal mine, which is where he had been heading.

By May of 1941 Clarke was forced to drop the whole Fan Mail "blog" due to the fact that he had been deprived of his typewriter while in basic training at Bridgenorth in Shropshire. However, this regrettable deprivation would not last for long.

One of his last transmissions went to Urania for the June issue in the form of an untitled commentary about how gravity waves might be propagated. By November he must have had his typewriter back because in that month's issue of Urania he wrote a lengthy and almost poetic review of Walt Disney's newly released *Fantasia*. Clarke was obviously emotionally moved and impressed by the movie and his review seems to evoke some of the ideas which would appear in another famous movie some 28 years later. *"The sun is in eclipse. Totality approaches and we wait for the appearance of the corona. As it flashes out in all its glory we move up and away from the earth, and the film ends with the great curve of the planet far beneath us and the pearly light of the corona in the sky. We have seen a thousand million years of the earth's history but Man is still in the far, far distant future."*

Just prior to the war and continuing until at least mid-1942 Clarke submitted letters, poetry and the odd article to Sam Youd's fanzine named *The Fantast*. Originally published by Youd in Hampshire it would be one of the few publications, along with the Futurian, to survive into the early war years. Clarke had originally encountered Youd through a very public disagreement in

Novae Terrae in October 1937. Youd had written an article attacking the trend of super-science stories now coming out of America, and he also contended that style in science fiction was not important. Clarke immediately rebutted Youd in the November issue with a piece titled *Science Fiction v Mr Youd*. This disagreement can't have lasted for long since Youd would not only fill in for Clarke by taking over his Fan Mail when his typewriter was confiscated, but also sportingly published a host of other Clarke essays between 1939-1941 before joining the Royal Signal Corps and being sent to Italy. (His magazine was then continued by another fan in Aberdeen, presumably even further away from the bombing). Clarke and Youd would become good friends and would correspond for many years after the war.

Clarke's poem *The Twilight of a Sun* was featured on the cover of the premier issue of The Fantast in April 1939. A short extract from the poem, *"For some day our vessels will fly to the uttermost depths of space,"* was accompanied by an image of a fleet of ships flying in space and a figure that appeared like a refugee from *Things to Come*. In the next issue Clarke wrote to Youd, *"Fancy that, I've got a cover at last! But I don't much care for the bloke on it ..."*

Despite the war, Clarke, Hanson, Temple, Turner and others all managed to write for The Fantast until mid-1942. Clarke concluded his contributions with a three-part parody named *A Short History of Fantocracy 1948-60*. This hilarious short story of a futuristic gathering of the BIS/SFA members describes Clarke and American super-fan Forrest Ackerman arriving via bomber at the Clarke farm in Somerset where they are met by Hanson, Turner and others.

In August of 1941 Clarke had been relocated to London where it was reported that he went and retrieved BIS documents from the wreckage of Bill Temple's house in Wembley. Nothing is known about what documents were so important to risk recovery during the blitz but we can probably assume that these materials still reside somewhere at BIS HQ. Two months later he was briefly back at the family farm having completed his RAF training. In January 1942 The Futurian reported, *"A letter from Arthur C. (Ego) Clarke, mad scientist of the B.I.S., informs us that he is now at No 2 RAF radio school as an instructor."*

In February 1942, despite reports that the society was now "in cold storage," BIS Organising Secretary Ralph Smith sent an article to *Flight* magazine with the latest revision of the BIS lunar spacecraft. In what must almost certainly have been an act of deliberate obfuscation and self-promotion Clarke and Val Cleaver (another BIS stalwart and Clarke's best friend) sent in letters of praise *and criticism* to Flight magazine which were printed in the next issue. One is left wondering whether the editor of Flight actually knew that these correspondents were alternately praising and criticising their own work!

During the same month Clarke sent a short story about suspended animation to Harry Turner for him to include in the February issue of his short-lived fanzine *Zenith*. Turner had managed to actually start his own fanzine in the early months of the war when his sign-up papers had been destroyed by the bombing of Manchester.

The following month Temple wrote to The Futurian: "*Dunno whether I mentioned it before, but I'm at Larkhill on Salisbury Plain, a couple of miles from Stonehenge. Ego (A.C. Clarke) is round about 20 miles away, I judge, at an RAF camp at Yatesbury. But the almost impassable wasteland of the vast artillery ranges lies between us, and so far we haven't been able to bridge it. I noticed the publicity the B.I.S. rocket ship has had recently, in Cassandra's column in the "Daily Mirror", in the London "Evening Standard", and of course in "Flight"? Good old Smithy! (Ralph Smith). He's doing this from his hospital bed, you know, where he's been stuck with a serious illness.*"

In November The Futurian featured a letter from Clarke headed, "*EGO REPORTS: You might like to know that I shall be appearing on the bookstalls as I have an article entitled "More Television Waveforms" in the November issue of "Electronic Engineering". It deals with the Fourier analysis of the exponential wave produced by the passage of rectilinear voltages through resistance-capacity couplings. Thought you'd like to know. Of more general interest, I should have a letter on the subject of interplanetary radio in the Nov. "Wireless World". They had an article on the subject last month and I made some comments on it which the editor said he would include in the next issue.*"

This is the first mention of Clarke corresponding with *Wireless World* about radio communications in space. He was responding to an article which had appeared in the October edition. Arthur's letter in the November 1942 issue challenged the notion that it would require six million kW to communicate by radio with another planet (something the editors had asserted.) He explained that it was not necessary to blanket the entire hemisphere to send such a signal, and that a beamed transmission would suffice. He concluded by stating that if the planet's atmosphere might be a hindrance to such a transmission it would be possible to set up UHF transmitters on a planet's "airless satellites." This seems to be the germ of a much bigger idea now formulating in his mind. Many years later Clarke mentioned that he may have been subconsciously influenced by science fiction writer George O. Smith who had written a series of stories about a set of interplanetary relay stations called *Venus Equilateral*. Smith's series first appeared at that exact time in the October issue of Astounding, which Clarke stated that he received from Willy Ley, the German rocket pioneer who had moved to America, "within weeks of publication." Smith would also work on radar and according to Clarke he was the first technically qualified writer to spell out the use of space stations for communications. The combination of the two things, the poorly written article in Wireless World and Smith's story in Astounding, seem to have triggered this first volley from Clarke about stations in space for radio communications.

Right next to the Wireless World story which had caught Arthur's attention, about communication through space, was another short article announcing the formation of The R.E.M.E. or the Royal Electrical and Mechanical Engineers. The boys' father, Charles Clarke, had been in the Royal Engineers. Shortly after this article appeared Fred joined the REME and was soon destined for Burma, South Africa and Sierra Leone (where Carnell had been sent.) The REME's job was to keep practically every piece of military hardware operational. According to his daughter Angie, Fred spent a lot of time "chasing the war;" and earned several commendations including the Burma Star.

Meanwhile, although Fred had departed for distant places Arthur remained in England with the radar "boffins" now down on Davidstow Moor in Cornwall, conducting his hair-raising experiments with the new, but still primitive, instrument guided landing and approach system. It would still be quite a few years before Arthur would venture abroad.

In May 1943 we hear, *"Sir Arthur Ego Clarke has at long last moved from Yatesbury, tearing up roots with reckless abandon on all sides and leaving three dozen bevies of weeping local maidens all-forlorn behind him."*

As the war raged on into 1943 Clarke went relatively quiet. One of his few reports to the community appeared in Futurian War Digest. Clarke said, *"I've now got my commission and am technical officer in charge of a pile of radio gear that would make any SF fan's hair stand straight upright. It makes mine do so anyway."*

Despite the BIS being in "cold storage" there were still other young enthusiasts willing to fill the void. Eric Burgess continued to keep his Manchester Astronautical Society functioning. Another group also sprouted in Farnborough, the legendary home of many experimental British aerospace endeavours. This was called the *Astronautical Development Society* and was run by Kenneth Gatland. All through 1941 Gatland and Burgess fought a spirited battle in the pages of Flight magazine against the rocket naysayers. This inevitably brought them together and in early 1944 the two organisations merged into the *Combined British Astronautical Societies* (CBAS). In late 1944 Clarke and Burgess made a trip to Wallasey, where Cleator lived, to discuss the future of astronautics in Britain. The result of their meeting was a policy statement encouraging the formation of a national astronautics organisation to be created after the war.

On January 20th 1945 Clarke attended a meeting in Islington between members of the CBAS and the old BIS. Clarke had maintained a file of the active members of the BIS and the people in that file had agreed to reunite after the war. All members were asked to write to a rendezvous address at the conclusion of hostilities. Almost immediately after the January summit the CBAS publication *Spacewards* featured a three page plea by Clarke called *The Ideal Astronautical Society*. In this essay Clarke explained why a post-war society needed to be national and *"have a name which expresses its purpose in a clear and if possible euphonious manner"*. He concluded that the old name of British Interplanetary Society should be used because it *"cannot be beaten, and in addition it is well known and its implications understood."*

Towards the end of the war Arthur Clarke unleashed a salvo of reviews and articles; beginning with *Rockets* (a review of Willy Ley's famous history of rocketry); *The Coming Age of Rocket Power* (a review of G. Edward Pendray's book of the same name); *The Astronomers New Weapons* (about radar astronomy); and *Extra-Terrestrial Relays*, his most famous paper which would ultimately change the world.

We have seen that the seed had been alive in his mind for nearly three years, but Clarke made his first unambiguous public reference to telecommunications satellites in a letter he sent to Wireless World magazine in February 1945. In this letter he combined the UHF transmitter with the stationary orbit (an idea which had also been around for at least thirty years.) His letter clearly stated *"An artificial satellite at the correct distance from the earth would make one revolution every 24 hours, i.e. it would remain stationary above the same spot..."* Over the next three months he would perfect the concept while stationed at Stratford-on-Avon (ironically the birthplace of one of England's greatest communicators, William Shakespeare). By 25th May 1945 it would be in the form of a small four-page booklet called *The Space Station – Its Radio Applications*. A month later he re-wrote the whole thing as *The Future of World Communications* and in August he submitted it for publication in October's Wireless World; whose editor then changed the name to *Extra-Terrestrial Relays*. Although many of the elements had been around for years the technology simply didn't exist to spell out the intellectual leap that Clarke would now propose. Clarke combined all of these old ideas with the new technology into one coherent plan which uniquely suggested that three satellites, 120 degrees apart, in a geosynchronous orbit, using beamed UHF transmission, could cover the entire planet with communications coverage. Clarke later stated that Eric Burgess developed the idea to its logical conclusion by proposing that the satellites be robotic and remotely controlled.

In the same letter to Wireless World Clarke also made mention of the German V2 rockets, which had not been used to go to the moon after all, but were falling from the skies all over England. In fact the very existence of the V2 spawned newspaper headlines in January 1945 to exclaim, *"German V-Bombs Revive U.K. Rocket-To-The-Moon"*, a reference to the BIS plans.

On the 9th of May Germany surrendered to the advancing allied forces and the war slowly ground closer to its ultimate conclusion. Many families had suffered terrible losses but thankfully the Clarkes had been spared the worst. Arthur's brother Fred was on his way home and so were most of his old BIS friends. The BIS had not yet regrouped so presumably in search of some stimulation Clarke attended one of the regular meetings of the *British Astronomical Association* (BAA). This group of amateur astronomers met every month in the Burlington Arcade just off Piccadilly in London. Some of the other alumni and lecturers at the BAA included Patrick Moore (who you will also hear from later in this book), Fred Hoyle and Sir Bernard Lovell. At a meeting on June 27th Clarke was officially inducted as a new member. He wasted no time in presenting a paper to the group but time didn't allow him to read it that night. It was titled *The Astronomer's New Weapons - Electronic Aids to Astronomy* and it was printed in the group's Journal for August. In this paper Clarke proposed the use of photo electric cells, arrayed in clusters, at a distance from one another, to compensate for atmospheric interference when taking astronomical images. This sort-of optical interferometer evokes the various advanced systems used today by both amateur and professional astronomers. *"Ultimately it may enable us to amplify images too faint to be recorded photographically, thus increasing the efficiency and effective aperture of our telescopes, with all that implies in cosmological research."*

Things proceeded fairly swiftly for the BIS throughout 1945. While Clarke was busy inventing the communications satellite Burgess continued to travel around the country meeting with all of the invested parties. On December 8th the entire amassed membership of all of Britain's aerospace groups rallied under the banner of the newly incorporated British Interplanetary Society. The two principle instigators, Burgess and Clarke, became official BIS members #1 and #2.

Having spent three years working on radar, a device that had literally helped win the war, Clarke considered other applications for this new technology. He even admitted later that he had tried to bounce a signal off the moon with an early radar set and had waited in vain for an echo. US Army signal corps engineers announced that they had successfully received echoes from the moon in January 1946, only to be told that the University of Sydney had accomplished the same result in 1941. In the March issue of the *Journal of the British Astronomical Association* he briefly discussed the US Army's experiments to bounce radar signals off the moon. Using his intimate knowledge of the systems used he was able to determine the power required and he concluded, *"The theoretical possibility of interplanetary radio communication is no longer open to doubt..."* Later he continued with more details and stated that *"(even) planetary ranges are now a distinct possibility."* He repeated this thought in the July issue of the Bulletin of the British Interplanetary Society and further explained the methods used by the US engineers for examining the moon. The same month he wrote a long explanation in Flight magazine of the radar assisted ground approach system he had worked on during the war. The following September he wrote a similar article for Wireless World.

By this time Flight Lieutenant A.C. Clarke was obviously in no mood to waste any time before exploiting the technological spoils of war. On October 5th he delivered a lecture to the BIS membership called *The Challenge of the Spaceship* in which he articulated his opinions about the reasons for space exploration. This paper would be singled out by the BIS membership in the years ahead as one of the most important papers ever given to the members. He compared the breaching of the space frontier as one of the four most important developments in human history joining along with the invention of agriculture, the taming of fire and the control of nuclear power. In keeping with his earlier combative approach to the naysayers he fired a few broadsides across the bows of noted author C.S. Lewis whose comments might well have represented the Challenge in the title of Clarke's paper. The Challenge of the Spaceship would continue to evolve as one of his most requested papers. The following year it would be anthologised in a book named "British Thought 1947."

In early 1947 Clarke wrote a two part article for *Aeroplane* magazine called *Principles of Rocket Flight*. The average British reader at this time would have become acquainted with the reality of rocketry, courtesy of the V2 bombardment of London. Although no one could any longer deny the existence of rockets capable of reaching into space, they still didn't fully comprehend how this was possible. Clarke's articles were easy to understand and covered most of the basic principles of spaceflight.

A month later he wrote a very high profile article in the *London Evening Telegraph*, it was titled *The First Men on the Moon* with the by-line *"by Arthur C. Clarke, former R.A.F. scientist, who was an original member of the British Interplanetary Society."* In this short essay Clarke addressed everything from the new science of hydroponics used for growing crops inside a moon base, to the use of nuclear power to open up the solar system. The same month an interview with Clarke appeared in the fanzine *Fantasy Review* in which he expressed his opinion that *"Space-travel will be here much earlier than any of us thought, Our most optimistic pre-war forecasts look very conservative now. Progress has been incomparably more swift than I dared hope for. I didn't expect to see jet propulsion so soon, and certainly not atomic energy. Things that looked as if they'd take a generation to develop are not only here, but obsolete already. I'm probably still being too pessimistic in putting the date of the first Moon trip at round about 1970."*

In September 1947 a modified version of The Challenge of the Spaceship would appear in the Toronto Star Weekly entitled *Will We Colonize Mars?* In this version Clarke discussed how we may need to modify the human frame to be able to live on other planets. He also spent some considerable time advocating the use of nuclear propulsion, *"A trip to Mars under atomic power need take only two or three weeks."* He then finished with his solution to interstellar travel with, *"... man will someday face this challenge. Perhaps he will answer it by the use of artificial planets, little self-contained worlds embarking upon journeys which would last for generations."*

In the December issue of the Journal of the British Astronomical Association Clarke's paper *Stationary Orbits* discussed the existence of two instances of natural near-stationary orbits, namely the Martian moon Deimos and one of the tiny moons of Jupiter. Both were almost at the exact radial distance to almost hang motionless above their host planets. In this same paper he also discussed the existence of the Lagrange points in the Earth-moon system and provided all the equations necessary to prove their existence. Clarke would write many short articles for the BAA and frequently attended the meetings in Piccadilly. Between 1945 and 1950 he would discuss gravitational lensing, neutron stars, Aerojet rocket experiments, meteor penetration and frequencies, cosmic background radiation, radio astronomy, the first radio maps of the galactic core, the anomaly in the constellation Cygnus, the calculation of meteor orbits using radar and the proof that many came from comets, the use of radio telescopes to calculate the surface temperature on the moon, the existence of a frozen surface on Ganymede, orbital refueling, atmospheric drag on spacecraft, orbital navigation using thrusters and gyros and many other topics which were almost all brand new subjects at the time Clarke wrote his observations.

On May 16th 1948 Clarke attended the first post-war gathering of British science fiction writers and editors, at a conference in London. He delivered a talk called *Science Fiction and Astronautics* in which he concluded that astronautics would not have developed so quickly without science fiction. He used the BIS as an example, *"There are a small minority of members who will not look at science fiction, a large number who read it surreptitiously and don't talk about it, and many who read and discuss it openly and don't give a damn what the rest think. These s-f fans are to be found among both technical and non-technical members."*

At this time Clarke was enrolled at *King's College* and was studying for his bachelor's degree in mathematics and physics. The success of one of his articles had been enough to secure a grant for him to attend the school in October of 1946. He graduated from King's College with first-class honours in August of 1948 and the story of his success would be reported in the local newspapers back in Somerset. It would be one of many such articles to appear in and around the Clarkes' hometown where he was rapidly evolving into a local hero. His brother Fred who had survived his foreign excursions was also making the local newspapers in Taunton. Fred had started a campaign to launch a Taunton "Model Parliament" to promote political awareness in the local youth community.

At this time Arthur was working at the *Institution of Electrical Engineers* as an assistant editor of Physics Abstracts. He would later state that he loved the job, "*...since every important journal in every language passed across my desk.*" He would stay at the IEE until his earnings from writing and talking on the radio began to surpass his salary. It would be his last job on a payroll.

In May of 1950 the headline "*Bishop's Lydeard Man Makes Television History*" announced that Clarke had delivered a 20 minute speech about the Fourth Dimension on the BBC. He had obviously been refining this presentation for some time, since he had first delivered it to the SFA back in August 1938. Apparently it was not historic because of the content, but because no one had ever done such a long speech on live television without interruption. The article went on to say that Clarke would be following up with another broadcast on space travel. When asked about the size of his audience (there were more TVs in England than in America at this time) Clarke quipped, "*I am used to lecturing and I realised that at most there would be only about five people watching me around each fireside.*" A viewer commented that, "*Mr Clarke had an extremely good television manner*".

Clarke's first book, *Interplanetary Flight*, would be published in 1950 by Temple Press, the same company that had published his articles in Aeroplane three years earlier. Impressive reviews began to appear in August and just a month later Clarke made his first trip abroad to attend the first *International Astronautical Congress* in Paris where he would strike up a life-long friendship with Fred Ordway (see later in this book.) Clarke evidently carried copies of his new book with him to help promote his status as a professionally published author. (Before the decade was over the newspapers would be announcing his 50th book. Many of these timeless volumes are also described in more detail further on in this book.) Arthur's brother Fred would also become a published author in the 1960s and even their mother Nora would ultimately write a book about raising the boys on the farm, named *My Four Feet on the*

Ground. Arthur later commented that she wrote at five times his speed and consequently he hoped she would avoid science fiction!

In October 1950 Clarke reviewed the movie *Destination Moon* for the BAA journal. He concluded with *"it will be a long time before the standard set by Destination Moon is excelled."* It would in fact be about 18 years and Clarke himself would be one of the instigators who raised the bar to new heights.

In May 1951 Carnell organized an *International Science Fiction* convention in London. It was on a scale previously unseen in England with over 200 attendees from around the world. From the original fourteen conventioneers Clarke, Mayer, Gillings, Johnson and Rosenblum attended. Other notable appearances from the pre-war crowd, referred to as "old time fans," were Sam Youd and Bill Temple. Clarke assumed his usual role of providing the accompanying music for the movies being screened, which led to a hilarious problem when at the last minute the choice of movie was changed. Clarke and Temple then struggled to provide a suitable musical backing for Conan Doyle's dinosaur fights. Later he provided the convention with a Technicolor screening of American rocket launches, which was apparently met with some enthusiasm. He also had his own small convention table where he was plugging his latest book *The Sands of Mars*. Clarke delivered a short speech to the attendees explaining the ludicrous makeup he had been obliged to wear to appear on the BBC. Apparently a peculiar dark green pancake had been used so that he wouldn't appear pasty white. Fred Clarke's wife Dorothy later recollected having to literally throw away the towels he had used to remove it.

In September Clarke and Burgess propelled the BIS plans into the big time when their ideas hit the front page of *The Illustrated London News*, one of the most widely read newspapers in England. The images showed a large satellite designed by Burgess and a diagram of Clarke's triangular three-satellite relay orbit. Further images showed the soon-to-be-familiar figure-eight flight plan to the moon and an astronaut on the moon in a BIS-designed spacesuit not entirely dissimilar to the later Apollo spacesuits.

In the March issue of yet another fanzine, *Science Fantasy News*, we can read the following: *"PICTURE POST ran A.C. Clarke article 'Liner to Mars' March 1st with full page 'ion rocket' technical illustration. COLLIERS intend to run an Interplanetary issue soon; watch for it."*

Picture Post was a British *Life* Magazine look-alike. In late 1951 Clarke had felt compelled to challenge a poorly written article which had appeared in the magazine. Needless to say he won that particular debate and was subsequently invited to write a remarkable short article unveiling plans for a titanic ion-propelled Mars-liner capable of carrying 1000 passengers and 260 crew on a two-month voyage to Mars. The accompanying image by Ralph Smith shows a toroidal vehicle spinning for artificial gravity with a large nuclear reactor poking out of the front.

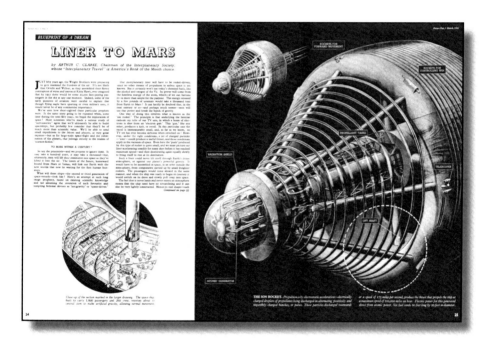

Clarke and Smith's gigantic ion-propelled Mars Liner as it appeared in Picture Post magazine, March 1st 1952. (Ralph Smith image courtesy BIS)

This sort of stupendously large engineering project is normally something attributed to Wernher von Braun, specifically in his book *The Mars Project*. Von Braun's propulsion expert Ernst Stuhlinger would not start to promote his own massive ion-propelled Mars vehicle until 1954. Clarke's fracas with

Picture Post had actually triggered his first written correspondence with Von Braun, who responded immediately and was more than happy to help Clarke win the debate. Perhaps coincidentally Von Braun would introduce his toroidal space station to an audience in Chicago literally two days after Clarke's article appeared in England.

Clarke knew exactly how ambitious this enormous spacecraft must have seemed to his post-war audience when he concluded, *"So much for our 1,000 passenger Queen Mary of Space, as far as we can imagine her, back here at the middle of the twentieth century. You, Sir, in the year 2500, poring over this microfilmed copy of Picture Post in the British Museum or the Mars Central Library—don't be too disdainful of our efforts, just because you know perfectly well that the Spacial Drive has been invented and rockets have followed the steam engine into oblivion! And don't think we're hopelessly conservative because we imagined that it would take two whole months to get to Mars!"*

In June, Clarke's book *The Exploration of Space* was published in England and America. It was chosen as the *Book of the Month* in the USA which immediately propelled Clarke to a new level of recognition. He soon found himself on the *Queen Mary* heading for New York for his first trip to America. Despite meeting almost every major player in space and science fiction during his trip, there was one particularly important exception; he didn't meet Wernher von Braun. At this time Von Braun had moved from White Sands in New Mexico to Huntsville Alabama and he was in the very early stages of a multi-year media campaign to promote the future of space exploration.

Before Clarke had left for America he must have compiled his own version of a media blitz for the British colour magazine *Illustrated*, which was being published from an office only 400 yards away from his old Grays Inn flat in London. While Clarke was still in America Illustrated began its four-issue series of his articles which provided a complete overview of the future of spaceflight; all accompanied by spectacular colour paintings rendered by legendary space artists Chesley Bonestell and Rolf Klep. Clarke was certainly aware of Bonestell's burgeoning reputation as the space artist *par excellence,* since his book *The Conquest of Space* (1949) had been awarded the first

International Fantasy Award for best Non-Fiction at Carnell's science fiction conference the previous summer. (Clarke's Exploration of Space would win in 1952.) In his review of the book Clarke said, *"No better introduction to astronautics could possibly be imagined"*. The Daily Express ran a three page feature on it. Bonestell had also just completed the motion picture Destination Moon with Robert Heinlein and he had been working with Willy Ley since at least 1945 painting various V2-shaped or bullet-shaped vehicles travelling to the Moon and Mars. In the July 1947 issue of *Mechanix Illustrated* Bonestell's Mars ships appeared side-by-side with the BIS Lunar lander. However, it seems to have been in March 1952 that both Von Braun and Clarke simultaneously began promoting massive space vehicles that substantially differed from the old V2 paradigm. Bonestell and Smith were only too happy to visualise them for publication.

Just days before Clarke had left for America the American magazine *Colliers* had begun its series of articles, using many of the same Bonestell and Klep images, but with text written by Von Braun, Willy Ley, Fred Whipple and others. The Colliers' series would be spread over two years and would play a huge role in publicizing space in America. The articles included *Man Will Conquer Space Soon, Man on the Moon, World's First Spacesuits*, and *Can We Get to Mars?* Clarke's four articles for Illustrated magazine were *Journey Into Space, The First Landing on the Moon, Pioneers in Space Suits* and *What Will We Find on Mars?* The campaigns on opposite sides of the Atlantic were startlingly similar and yet the first Colliers' article wasn't even announced until four weeks before Clarke left for America and his entire four-part series ran in England before he returned home in August. Even making allowances for a copy of the first Colliers making the journey across the Atlantic before Clarke left for America it seems extremely unlikely that he would have thrown together an entire magazine series in the few days before leaving. The second part of the Colliers series didn't appear until two months after Clarke returned to England and didn't conclude until 1954 with Von Braun's version of a giant Mars fleet. It is unknown what interaction, if any, led to this largely forgotten trans-Atlantic synchronicity.

The same day that Clarke's articles began in England his face also appeared on the front cover of the *Saturday Review*, one of the most widely read magazines in the United States. Inside the magazine appeared a review of The Exploration of Space written by none other than Fred Whipple, who generally approved of the book, but took Clarke to task about some of his riskier predictions. Strangely, the one prediction that Whipple contested the most, the existence of lunar ice, has of course since been proven to be true. Also rather amusingly Whipple noted that the pictures in Clarke's book couldn't compete with those by Bonestell. Perhaps this was a sly bit of promotion by Whipple for the Colliers' series; but unbeknownst to Whipple the Bonestell images to which he was referring were appearing next to the Clarke by-line in England at that exact moment.

The Saturday Review – Exploration of Space cover 1952

Some of Clarke's predictions in The Exploration of Space have yet to manifest themselves, but it is apparent that he would not allow himself to commit what he later described as a failure of nerve or a failure of imagination; two grave sins frequently perpetrated by other "experts" on astronautics.

Clarke would set up one of his slide shows on his return to England. At the December meeting of the BAA he told the gathered membership all about his three months in America. He had spent time at the Bell laboratories in New Jersey where he got his first look at the "famous transistors" which he estimated would *make possible computing machines of a smallness and efficiency never before imagined.* He told them of his time with Robert Heinlein followed by a visit with Clyde Tombaugh. He then went on to Los Angeles and visited the set of *War of the Worlds* which George Pal was just finishing. But his most memorable moment seems to have been staring into the maw of the giant 200-inch telescope at Mount Palomar. On this occasion his slide show was met with enthusiastic applause by the members on hand.

Demand for Clarke in America soon led to more frequent sojourns across the Atlantic. During one of these trips he went on a scuba diving expedition to Florida where he met a beautiful young American single mother named Marilyn Mayfield. Clarke said that sparks flew immediately and within a few weeks the two were married in a quiet ceremony in New York. Unfortunately many factors contributed to the marriage only lasting a few months. The couple barely knew each other. Clarke was insular and hard working, often spending days at a time barely communicating while he wrote. Marilyn had been used to the warmth and vibrancy of Florida and didn't easily adapt to England or being left alone for long periods of time. Clarke later admitted that the marriage was "incompatible from the beginning." After stating that everyone should marry once, Clarke would never marry again.

In May 1953 the newly revised version of The Challenge of the Spaceship would appear in the highly prestigious United Nations' journal *Impact of Science on Society* and Clarke's words would be quoted around the world. One newspaper noted that the publication of Clarke's article might well *"be the first time the United Nations has paid any attention to (spaceflight)."* Clarke had removed many things from his original 1946 draft. Gone were the references to the Peenemunde rocketeers; his gentle condemnation of C.S. Lewis and his

warnings against interplanetary imperialism. However, he added the promise of nuclear powered ion engines and drew attention again to the inevitability of communication satellites. The UNESCO people would reprint the paper at least twice more, once immediately after Sputnik and then immediately after the Apollo 11 moon landing usually with some sort of editorial comment about how Clarke was so far ahead of his time.

As his reputation grew, Clarke would not neglect his friends at New Worlds magazine. After one failed attempt shortly after the war, the magazine was successfully reborn under Carnell's and then Moorcock's, stewardship and became one of the most widely read science fiction magazines in British history.

In the four years immediately following the war Carnell only managed to publish five issues, mainly because of power outages and paper shortages, but Clarke was still there. In the third issue, in October 1947, his short story *Inheritance* made its first appearance under the pseudonym of Charles Willis. One of the most remarkable things about Inheritance is that it reads like a flight report from the late 1950s X-15 program. There are a number of references to Wales and Welsh characters, undoubtedly left over from his time at Colwyn Bay, and Clarke even refers to himself as an astronaut-in-waiting; but most noteworthy are the descriptions of suborbital launches, staging problems (exactly as experienced 15 years later by Yuri Gagarin), dauntless rocket-plane pilots, radar tracking and recovery operations. At the *exact same time* that Carnell published Clarke's tale of rocket-jockeys a young captain named Charles Yeager broke the sound barrier for the first time in an experimental rocket plane at Muroc air field in California. Less than a year later, Clarke sold the story to John Campbell in America for Astounding Magazine.

In early 1949 in Carnell's fifth issue of New Worlds, Clarke's article called *The Shape of Ships to Come* first articulated his opinions on the best shape for a long range spacecraft. After explaining the advantages of nuclear propulsion he wrote, *"Heavy shielding would therefore be necessary to protect the crew. Atomically propelled spaceships will be long and thin...with the crew chamber at one end and the motors at the other...our private guess, at this time of writing is that they might be dumbbell shaped...(one) sphere would contain the crew, cargo and fuel...the smaller would hold the atomic engines as well as the radiation shielding."* This design, or something just like it, would propagate for the next two decades; it would be pictured in Clarke's first book in 1950, followed by Flight magazine in 1951, then it would reappear as the Boeing company's 1959 deep space exploration vessel known as *PARSECS*, which would, in turn, bear an uncanny resemblance to the spacecraft in a certain science fiction movie just nine years after that.

Clarke's "The Sentinel" as it appeared on the cover of New Worlds in 1954
(Courtesy - Michael Moorcock)

Speaking of THAT movie; next to his non-fiction essay, Extra-Terrestrial Relays, arguably the most significant creation in Clarke's oeuvre would be the short story *The Sentinel* which was originally written for a competition held by the BBC in 1948. This short story would see first publication in 1951, in a one-off science fiction magazine called *Ten Story Fantasy*, then in his book *Expedition to Earth* in 1953, before finally gracing the cover of issue number 22 of Carnell's now-professionally produced New Worlds, in 1954. Few Clarke fans are unaware that this is the story he later sold to Stanley Kubrick and would become one of the direct influences for the motion picture *2001: A Space Odyssey*. The Sentinel's impact would also not be forgotten by an impressionable young American science fiction fan and aspiring actor named Keir Dullea who you will hear from later in this book.

By 1954 Clarke was appearing regularly in magazines and newspapers all over England and America. A three-part series appeared in *Everybody's* magazine called *Conquest of the Moon*. Clarke would pull out all the stops with the help of Ralph Smith, who would fill the pages with his astonishing art of lunar landers, rovers, moon bases and lunar observatories. *Everybody's* was a long-running mainstream tabloid read by, well...nearly everybody. The article was specifically designed to promote the new book by Smith and Clarke called *The Exploration of the Moon*.

Arthur C. Clarke and Wernher von Braun in the late 1960s.

Just as Wernher von Braun had unleashed his campaign of books, magazines and films with Colliers and Walt Disney in America; Clarke, Burgess, Smith and the other BIS members were using the same techniques to convince the British public that people would be going to the moon within their lifetimes. Unfortunately, unlike Von Braun, they were in the wrong country to be able to implement their grand designs.

Clarke's success allowed him to start travelling around the world. On June 30th 1954 he was in a decompressed DC4 aircraft at 13,500 feet above Hudson's Bay in Canada. He was with forty other reporters and enthusiasts awaiting a total eclipse of the sun. When the moment of totality arrived he was looking out of the wrong side of the plane examining the progress of the moon's shadow. When he stumbled in the dark to the right side of the plane he observed *"the sky was not black, but a very deep blue and I saw no stars... we all felt like excited schoolboys because everything had worked so perfectly."*

Around this time Clarke would meet Mike Wilson at one of his social group's many pub gatherings in London. Wilson was well travelled and invited Clarke to go on a scuba diving expedition on the far side of the globe. This invitation would lead Arthur to his future home in Sri Lanka. The country was beautiful, the diving was spectacular and the climate was a lot better than London where Arthur had been living with his brother Fred and Fred's wife Dorothy. Arthur's passion for scuba diving would lead him to start a business with Mike Wilson and ultimately from there into film making. Clarke would initially share a bungalow in the suburbs of Colombo with Wilson and his wife Elizabeth.

At the end of the 1950s, Clarke would be seen by millions of people on television as he spoke from the stage at London's festival hall; in the company of the Duke of Edinburgh. He took that opportunity to again plug the notion of satellite television and also in a moment of uncharacteristic pique he took a jab at the cold-warmongers with, *"...there is enough energy in a single H-bomb explosion to send the entire British Navy to Mars and back."*

Back in 1956 Clarke had met a young boxer named Hector Ekanayake. Clarke and Hector became good friends immediately and when Arthur sustained a serious head injury in 1962 Hector took on the role of his caregiver while he recovered. This injury would forestall Clarke's plans to continue the recovery of a ship load of sunken Persian treasure that he and Wilson had discovered off the coast of Sri Lanka. In a letter to a friend at the time Clarke wrote, *"I'm afraid the treasure hunting expedition had to be postponed, but as it's waited two hundred and fifty years, one more won't make much difference."*

The relationship with Hector Ekanayake would evolve into a business partnership and would last for the next fifty years. When it became apparent that Arthur's mother couldn't be cared for adequately in Sri Lanka his brother Fred chose to leave London and return to Taunton to take care of Nora. Hector's wife and kids would become Arthur's surrogate family in Sri Lanka and would be there at his side for the rest of his life. (More of Arthur's life in Sri Lanka is described further on in this book by Nalaka Gunawardene.)

Clarke would submit many more stories and articles to New Worlds over the next ten years and in 1962 he would return to his post as editor for a special edition on Yuri Gagarin. A photograph of Clarke on the front cover shows him positively beaming with excitement as he stands in front of the first man in space, who is holding one of Clarke's books. In August of that same year the *Daily Mail* reported that Clarke had returned from his home in Sri Lanka to no fanfare from his countrymen. *"Arthur C. Clarke...is the 44-year-old scientist whose idea made Telstar possible. American engineers have paid tribute to his work. There was no welcome for him – just a family reunion with his brother in a semi-detached house at Bowes Park in North London."* However, a year later, on returning again to Somerset, a party was held in his honour at his old school. The science teacher at the dinner stated, *"In giving you this toast of Arthur Clarke I feel that I am giving you the toast of a science fiction writer who has already outdistanced H.G. Wells and a scientist who is likely to be regarded as one of the outstanding men of science of the present day."*

Clarke had found his place amongst the great pioneers of space exploration. The young gangly boy from Minehead with the big dreams had come a long way and yet he was only just beginning.

Science Fiction – Past, Present and Future

(Novae Terrae - June 1937)

by Arthur C. Clarke

It is commonly asserted by science-fiction fans, and by editors of science-fiction magazines wishing to increase their circulation, that their peculiar brand of literature has in the past exerted a considerable influence on scientists and inventors by suggesting new lines of development which have been followed up to produce epoch-making results. They would, for example, praise Jules Verne as the inspirer or originator of such mechanical achievements as the airplane and the submarine. Somehow this attitude seems altogether too enthusiastic.

Although in many of his tales, Verne quite accurately predicted the course of future invention, it seems improbable that he can be considered responsible for the later fulfilment of his own stories. The airplane and the submarine would have been invented if "The Clipper of the Clouds" and "Twenty Thousand Leagues Under the Sea" had never been written. It is the influence of the social background of the time that is primarily responsible for both science-fiction story and invention; it is seldom that the story produces the invention, although the reverse may often happen.

In the opinion of the writer, for what it is worth, the real use – apart from its entertainment value – of scientific fiction in the past has been in preparing people's minds for coming changes and discoveries. If invention after invention were to burst unheralded upon an unsuspecting world, the effect would in time be devastating. Thanks to the science-fiction story, those people whose minds are less acrobatic and elastic than that of the average 'fan', have a chance to get used to ideas, which had they come suddenly, might have completely upset their mental equilibrium. Grandfather may never have believed that man would fly, any more than father thinks that one day little Tommy will be wandering across the Mare Imbrium carefully ignoring the "Rubbish Here, Please" notices of the Lunar Anti-Litter Society. But when the first space ships begin their deafening onslaught upon the Empyrean, the people who start removing the cotton wool from their ears after the last concussion has echoed down from the stratosphere will have been used to the idea all their lives.

In this case, perhaps for the first time, science fiction authors have actually influenced future development to no small extent, and when space is eventually crossed – which I venture to predict will be somewhat earlier than the appearance of a printed issue of "Novae Terrae" – science fiction will have played an enormous part in the final development of the space ship, which is now almost completed, science fiction authors and engineers have derived mutual benefit from the work of each other. Indeed, often the author has turned engineer or the engineer has left the work-bench for the typewriter, as in the cases of Valier, Manning, Pendray, Ley and Cleator. The engineer creates some new device, and the author tests its functioning by incorporating it in a story. Should there be anything wrong with the idea; a myriad furious fans very quickly draw attention to the fact. As a substitute to an actual trial, which is usually impossible at the moment, this procedure may give very useful results. Think of the storm over "The Irrelevant", which I have no doubt cleared away many dynamical cobwebs from the minds of would-be astronauts who had not realized that although the same laws of motion and energy hold everywhere, we sue particular forms of them here on earth and must not forget it.

The public gets practically all of its ideas about space flight from science-fiction stories and for that reason any gross errors in such stories should be dealt with neatness and dispatch. (There are those who say that Paul Ernst should have been slowly dehydrated for "The World Behind the Moon". Personally, I think that complete ionization was indicated.) The Interplanetary Societies recruit their members chiefly from the ranks of science fiction readers, and it would probably be an underestimate to say that inveterate fans make up seventy-five per cent of their total numbers. When space is eventually conquered, it will be science fiction's greatest triumph.

It might be thought that when we have reached the nearer planets, authors will no longer write stories about them for fear that the discovery of new facts will soon make their tales ridiculous. What is much more probably, however, is that interplanetary travel will give authors a whole host of themes for their plots. For every fact that we shall discover about Mars there will be a hundred intriguing mysteries, and the science fiction author will not be slow to take advantage of them. He will always be one stop ahead of the scientist, writing stories about Jupiter when we are clambering around the asteroids, letting his imagination run riot on Pluto when the first ship is circling Neptune.

Is it too disrespectful to think of the science fiction author as the carrot that is dangled in front of the donkey-scientist to lure him on to ever greater efforts? With it the author will entice him from Proxima Centauri to the Clouds of Magellan at the edge of the first universe, and then on to the neighbouring galaxies floating in space just a little further away. After that, onwards to the farthest nebulae, a thousand million light years out, that appear as faint smudges with the greatest telescopes on Earth. Not until the cosmos has been circumnavigated will the story be ended, and how long that will take no man of today can imagine. Then, and only then, will the science fiction author, should he still exist in what we hope will be an otherwise perfect universe, find his activities somewhat curtailed.

But before him will still stretch the Future and the frail vessel of man's imagination will venture forth into the uncharted wastes of this ocean, just as untold ages before, he first sailed the seas of tiny earth, and, a very little while later, crossed the gulfs of space to the other planets of the sun.

The British Fan in his Natural Haunts - Arthur C. Clarke

(Novae Terrae June 1938)

by William F. Temple

Arthur Clarke and his Ego live alone in a tiny divan bd stg. rm., h & c. rnng. Wtr., use of bth.-rm., in a house in Norfolk Square, W.2. The smallness of this room is a standing joke in the London Branch SFA – there is a tale that Arthur once wore a double-breasted suit for the first time and got wedged between the walls for three days. So, when one beery evening at the A.O.D. Arthur invited me to examine it, I accompanied him eagerly.

We toiled up many flights of stairs; A. lives on the top floor. (Funny how these astronomers like the roof.) At last we stood outside the door of the famous den. A. (hereinafter called "A.") flung open the door with a magnificent gesture, snapped down the electric light switch, and thundered "Behold!" But the effect was somewhat spoiled for he'd forgotten to leave a lamp in the light-socket, and the room remained obstinately in darkness. However he advanced boldly into the gloom, fumbled about and found the lamp (and a few other things by the sound of it) and had another go: "Behold!"

But again an anti-climax. My fault this time. I wasn't there. You see, I'd noticed a small room on the stairs and had to retreat there urgently. It had been a very beery evening in the A.O.D. Still, I came panting back again commendably quickly, and at last entered the sanctum. Only just though. For there was hardly room for the two of us, and A's ego had to be left outside on the landing. A. himself generously opened the window and sat himself half outside it to allow me to look around freely.

Pinned on the wall was a yard-square photo of the Moon. Actually it was made up of four smaller sections, each of different sizes and parts, and the consequence was a moon that bulged badly in the wrong places, and one hemisphere missed the other completely and stuck out into space for several hundreds of miles. But A. knew his craters and mapped them out as I indicated them: "Tycho, Aristulus, Copernicus....." "What's this?" I asked, pointing out a strange, straight mark in the Alps. "The Great Cleft" answered A. promptly. "Queer thing – there's no debris in or around it. It's dead straight, too. Like the slash of an atomic ray gun."

"Ha! Let's get onto science fiction then. What's your favourite story?"

"One I wrote myself" interpolated the Ego, poking its head round the door. I batted it one and it retired with an even more swollen head than usual. With true scientific indetermination A. couldn't decide upon his favourite story. I caught sight of more books piled on top of his cupboard and brought them down in a shower of sugar and grape-nuts – did I mention that A's larder is on top of the cupboard too? The first book I looked at was "The Moon" by Professor Pickering. Impatiently I threw it aside and picked up the next. It was entitled "The Moon" by Nasmyth and Carpenter. "Heck!" I said and picked up the next. Yes, it was titled "The Moon" – this time by Nielson. I gave it up.

"You B.I.S. Moonatic" I said "haven't you anything else less technical?"

replied "My library is at Taunton, my home-town. It contains complete sets of WONDER, ASTOUNDING, about 100 science fiction novels and more than 100 books of pure science."

"Darned if I'm going to Taunton (if there is such a place) to check up on it" I said. "So I'll have to take your word for it."

Here A's conscience smote him.

"Well; to tell you the truth, my ASTOUNDING collection is two short," he mumbled. The Ego thrust its head into the room at this, and gave A. such a look of utter contempt that the poor fellow blushed.

"A fine chance to boost yourself without being detected – and you throw it away you weak twirp!" it remarked bitterly. And withdrew.

I made another desperate attempt to make something of the books A. had with him, and picked up a read one. It was "A Mathematical Theory of Relativity" by Koppf.

"Dammit, this is a bit too steep," I grumbled. "Can't you remember what books you've got at Taunton, wherever that is?"

"I keep a list. That's the best of having a methodical mind" answered A. brightly, yanking a drawer open.

I've never seen such a jumbled clutter of bric-a-brac as was in that drawer – buttons, pins, stamps, the B.I.S. cash box, cutlery, pamphlets, wool (A. darns his own socks), sardine-cans, tram-tickets, bits of well-worn chewing gum – everything came flying out as the methodical mind searched for its list. There were, too, I remember, thick files of letters from Sam Youd and Eric Frank Russell, and an especially thick file of carbon copies of letters written by A. himself. This last file was, I learned, the Ego's favourite reading material on Sunday afternoons.

At last the list. It was an exercise book printed neatly at first, and then degenerating into A's wildest scribble as it went on. Against the title was A's ratings. "F", "G". "V.G." etc. There were all the familiar titles known to every s-f fan, and many that were new to me, such as Lance Sieveking's "Stampede" (illustrated by G.K. Chesterton) and Beresford's "Gods of the Purple Planet". A. wouldn't venture to name his favourite book, but I noticed that though "V.V.G." (very, very good) was not uncommon; against Stapledon's "Star-Maker" was just one word "Superb."

I had another glance around the room. There was a microscopic radio set in the cupboard – there was no room for it outside. But that was O.K., for A. when lying in bed could swing the cupboard door with his foot, thus regulating the volume of sound. It occurred to me rather belatedly that I ought to include a personal portrait of A. in the interview. So I looked at him. One must take the bad with the good in a reporter's life.

I beheld a tallish, rather clever-looking fellow (appearances are deceptive) whose eyes glinted at me through horn-rims with a condescending expression. He looks as if he hopes he looks like a scientist, does A. His hair cannot make up its mind whether it is dark or fair, is perfectly dry, and sticks up like a wire-brush. An over-zealous barber wandered about in it for days, and when the search-party found him told an astounding story which A. used as a plot for one of his yarns.

He's impatient and highly-strung, and says he's not, and given to sudden violent explosions of mirth (mostly at his own jokes). This is sometimes embarrassing to we fans who meet in Lyons (Ed: a Holborn pub) on Thursday evenings, and when he rolls on the floor convulsed in mad mirth we pretend he isn't with our party, and wonder why the manageress allows these queer people in. The bowls are soon empty of lump sugar on our table too, for A. eats pounds of it, ever since he heard that diabetic persons (e.g. H.G. Wells) are intellectually clever on the average.

While I was thus ruminating A. suddenly heard the call of the sugar-bowl, and invited me out to supper. So we tucked the Ego in the little bed (it was its turn tonight) A. was sleeping in the wash-bowl) and went to the café on the corner, and had some lump sugar and crumbly sausage rolls. I had to pay for myself. I still don't know where Taunton is, but now I suspect it is somewhere in Scotland.

Postscript to the above: While they were still in blissful ignorance about this article A. and his Ego decided to share a flat with me at No. 88 Gray's Inn Road W.C. 1. I take this opportunity to point out that I will not hold myself responsible for any debts incurred by them or myself either, and also to record these last words should there be murder in Holborn when this issue of "N.T." appears: I did what I did according to my lights (my liver being out of order at the time.)

William F. Temple, Arthur Clarke's room-mate and first biographer
(Courtesy: Anne and Joe Patrizio)

IMPORTANT ANNOUNCEMENT.

(Advertisement in Novae Terrae August 1938)

We have the pleasure in announcing that Messrs. Clarke and Temple are throwing open their "den" in their flat for use as a London clubroom for all SFA members each Thursday evening from 6 pm onwards. The address is 88 Grays Inn Road W.C. 1. (The entrance is a few yards below the junction of Grays Inn Road and Theobald's Rd towards Holborn. Look for the sign over the door, "FOOT CLINIC.") This arrangement starts Thurs. Aug 18th. It is hoped to transfer the library to the den shortly. No business will be transacted at these meetings: they are informal, and for fostering acquaintance between members. Please bring your own sandwiches, chocolate, booze etc., if you wish to feed on the premises. All members who can get to these weekly meetings are genuinely welcome.

The British Fan - William F. Temple

(Novae Terrae January 1939)

by Arthur C. Clarke

As I write this the author of "The Smile of the Sphinx", "Lunar Lilliput," etc., etc., etc., is prowling around the room in eccentric circles pushing the carpet sweeper before him. Ever and anon he sends a reproachful glance in my direction, but it produces absolutely no effect. (My conscience is clear: didn't I wipe up the crockery? If you don't believe me, look in the dustbin.) Every time it reaches perihelion the sweeper gives a gargling click and disgorges a pile of dust, tram tickets, gramophone needles, and cigarette ends. On the next circuit it picks them up again, and so the pile of cosmic debris travels on through space, engulfing planet after planet, sun after sun – Sorry, wrong story.

The carpet sweeper has left the room now, clucking like a Gieger-Muller counter about to lay an egg, and I can write without fear of an inquisitive nose snooping over my shoulder. So now's the time for a few personalities. Moderately tall, moderately dark, immoderately unhandsome, Bill works in the stock exchange, which doesn't suit him one little bit. He was trained for some years to be an engineer but dropped that, and now he doesn't know the difference between a double jointed, waffle-nosed cam and an eccentrically pivoted bi-phase fluking iron (the ignorant fellow!) The only things he does know something about are films, Douglas Fairbanks (Sen.), H.G. Wells, appendicitis (tummy-ache to you) and rejection slips. He says he's got a bad temper, but hasn't, and says he doesn't like writing, but does.

When he wants to write he retreats to his room, where he has a writing bureau full of Dictionaries and Thesauruses (Thesauri?). If it's cold, he lights an oil stove, and has to emerge every half hour for a breath of fresh air. This gives him an excuse to stop work, and he generally makes the best of it. Every few weeks he swears solemnly: "Next week I'll start writing in earnest" and when the week comes, he either spends every night at the flicks or else crawls from pub to pub trying to drown a set of practically unsinkable sorrows. If anyone ever films his life, they'll call it "The Birth of Procrastination."

One thing I like about this chap Temple is the clarity of his mind and the way he concentrates his activities into a few narrow fields in order to obtain the maximum efficiency. This is shown very clearly in his library – I'll select a few books at random: "Houdini's Escapes," "The Film Till Now," "Bulldog Drummond," "The British Landscape," "The Appeal of Jazz," "How to Concentrate," Coleridge's Poems, "Expressions of the Emotions in Man and Animal," "Autobiography of a Journalist," "Outline of History," "Angel Pavement." Could specialisation go further? It's the same with his 300-odd records: when you find the Adagio from Grieg's Pianoforte Concerto in A Minor nestling beside Judy Garland singing "It Never Rains," you can be sure you have come across a logical, incisive mind that will let no obstacle come between it and its goal....if only it could decide what its goal was.

Bill doesn't go in for s-f very heavily nowadays. His depleted file of s-f mags turns into a collection of "Film Weeklies" after a year or two. The only mag. of which he has a good collection is TALES OF WONDER. He has 15 copies of no. 4....So he doesn't know a thing about real s-f as epitomized by Repp, Hamilton, Kuttner and Schachner. Richard Seaton is just a name to him, and he thinks Hawk Carse was a dealer in second-hand Fords.

On the mantelshelf stand two of his proudest possessions: autographed photos of Eleanor Powell and Douglas Fairbanks (Sen.). In the middle, H.G. Wells sits on top of my midget radio, and hops about in a most un-Wellsian manner when the six pips come through. All attempts to make Bill remove these photos (which lower the whole moral tone of our establishment) have so far failed. We admit the necessity for Wells, even if he does look as if that diabetes is coming on again, but Miss Powell and Doug. Fairbanks (Sen.) – I mean to say!

I've mentioned that he's very interested in films; he has a projector (of sorts) and once ran through some Fairbanks (Sen.) films before we put a stop to it. One of his six or seven ambitions is to be a film director, so we may yet see "The Smile of the Sphinx" screened under the title "Enough to Make a Cat Laugh." He's also very interested in Astronautics, and as Publicity Director of the British Interplanetary Society writes screeds to the B.B.C. and anyone else who's likely to help the good cause.

I had better hurry up and finish this, as I hear him coming back again, rolling the dustbin down the stairs. One thing I've forgotten to tell you about him is his habit of getting up 5 minutes before he is due to leave for work in the morning, and his miserable habit of constant pessimism, his excruciating whistle and neurotic...

(Editor's note:- The above manuscript was discovered among the literary effects of the late Arthur C. Clarke, who was found battered to death with a carpet sweeper in his flat some weeks ago. We publish these last words from his brilliant and versatile pen as an indication of the great loss that has been suffered by the worlds of literature, art, science, etc., etc., and etc., De mortuis nil nisi bonum....)

Arthur - July 1940

Fred, Nora and Arthur Clarke

88 Gray's Inn Road as it is today, top floor flat was where Arthur lived in the 1930s

Arthur C. Clarke visiting The British Interplanetary Society

Chapter III - Friends and Followers

Arthur C. Clarke: a Friend to Love and Admire

by Frederick I. Ordway III

I've known Arthur since September 1950 when my new wife Maruja and I were in Paris. We had left New York on the French Line's Liberté on the 14th of September, arrived in Le Havre on the 20th, and soon settled into quarters on Rue de Longchamps in the 16th arromdissement. On arrival we learned that on the 29th the world's first International Astronautical Congress would be taking place in the Grand Amphitheatre de la Sorbonne on the rue des Écoles. The cost for admittance: 150 francs

We immediately enrolled, I as a long-time member of the American Rocket Society. It was there in Paris, at and following the opening ceremonies, that I met and soon became a friend and colleague of Arthur C. Clarke. We chatted, kept in touch following the congress, and I was then guided into membership of the British Interplanetary Society in which Arthur served as executive secretary.

Not long thereafter Arthur sent me copies of his "Interplanetary Flight: An Introduction to Astronautics" (London, 1950: Temple Press) and "The Exploration of Space" (London, 1951: Temple Press). I was thrilled!

Over the years we would meet in the States, in England, and at various international congresses. My wife and I met Arthur's wife Marilyn, his brother Fred, and other family members and I would enthusiastically write articles for the Journal of the British Interplanetary Society and other publications. A bond grew over the years, even though Arthur's health obliged him to live in far away Sri Lanka. I continued to collect his books and he on occasion would supply commentary to mine, notably a foreword to "Intelligence in the Universe (Prentice-Hall, 1966) and an epilogue to "Blueprint for Space" (Smithsonian Institution Press, 1992).

Then came an entirely unexpected reunion. It all began in January 1965. I was in New York with my colleague Harry H-K Lange attending meetings with our publishers. At one of these meetings someone mentioned that my old friend Arthur C. Clarke was in town. I knew Arthur always stayed at the Chelsea Hotel on 23rd Street and so I rang him at the first opportunity. He answered and we promptly set up a reunion at the Harvard Club where I always stay while visiting New York.

As we brought each other up to date on our recent activities, I learned that Arthur was in the city to publicize his recent "Man and Space" book published by Time, Inc. and to discuss doing a film with director Stanley Kubrick.

It soon became apparent that we were both simultaneously involved with the theme of intelligence in the universe, the title of my book with Harry Lange's illustrations was "Life in Other Solar Systems" (Dutton, 1965) and the other was "Intelligence in the Universe" whose proofs we had turned over to Prentice-Hall that very week. It was the same theme that Kubrick and Clarke were planning to cover, inspired by Arthur's short story "The Sentinel" published some 15 years earlier.

Time was running out. We all had evening engagements, but shortly after leaving the club Clarke contacted Kubrick who then called me, introducing himself by saying "I am Stanley Kubrick." He proposed a get together, the four of us, Clarke, Kubrick, Lange and Ordway. This occurred on the 23rd of January 1965 in Kubrick's apartment on the East Side of Manhattan.

What followed was an exciting collaboration that started in New York and months later moved to the MGM British Studios in Borehamwood, north of London. The film "2001: A Space Odyssey" would premier three years later at the Uptown Theatre in Washington, D.C.

Arthur and I stayed in contact in the years that followed our "2001" adventure with Stanley Kubrick. Our last literary collaboration occurred in 2005 when we worked with Anthony Frewin on "Are We Alone?--The Stanley Kubrick Extraterrestrial-Intelligence Interviews" (Eliott & Thompson, London, 2005). Arthur provided the preface and I the afterword. A grateful Tony Frewin wrote, "Fred, Wouldn't have been possible without you!" --and of course Arthur, and Stanley, and all the distinguished people we interviewed for "2001" that were never shown as originally planned as a preface to the film--a disappointing cancellation for many of us involved with "2001."

I have proudly served on the Arthur C. Clarke Foundation that has recently led to the Arthur C. Clarke Center for the Human Imagination at the University of California at San Diego. Arthur may no longer be with us but his name, personality, accomplishments and vision will remain for eons.

Frederick I. Ordway III is a space scientist and well-known author of visionary books on spaceflight. Ordway was in charge of space systems information at the Marshall Space Flight Center from 1960 to 1963. He was a professor at the University of Alabama's School of Graduate Studies and Research. He was technical consultant to the film 2001: A Space Odyssey. Ordway was educated at Harvard and completed several years of graduate study at the University of Paris and other universities in Europe.

Arthur C. Clarke

by Michael Moorcock

I was a very young journalist, of 17 or so, when Arthur C. Clarke invited me to celebrate his birthday before he returned to Ceylon, where he had recently settled. The party was scheduled for November 5th in North London. Flattered to be asked, I reluctantly gave up plans to get drunk and do exciting things with explosives and set off into the terra incognita of Tottenham where Arthur's brother Fred lived a modest and respectable life. A bottle in my pocket, I knocked at the door to be greeted by Fred. "It's round the corner," he said. "I'm just off there myself." He turned a thoughtful eye on the bottle. "I don't think you'll need that."

"Promising", I thought. Ego (Arthur's nickname since youth) has laid everything on. I let Fred place the bottle on the hallstand and followed him for a few hundred yards through misty streets, determinedly re-enacting the Blitz with Roman Candles and Catherine Wheels, until we arrived at a church and one of those featureless halls of the kind where the Scouts held their regular meetings. Sure enough, inside was a group of mostly stunned friends and acquaintances holding what appeared to be teacups, one of which was shoved into my hand as I was greeted by Arthur in that Somerset-American accent that was all his own. "Welcome," he said. "Got everything you want?"

"Um," I stammered. "Is there only tea?"

"Of course not!" beamed the mighty intelligence, who had already published the whole concept of satellite communication on which our modern world is based, "there's orange juice, too." He indicated a serving hatch. "But you'd better hurry, Mike. The film show's starting soon." I noticed that ladies of the kind who help out at church socials were organizing chairs. I strolled up to Ted Carnell who, in the 30s, had founded New Worlds (Novae Terrae) with Arthur and John Wyndham when it was still a mimeographed fanzine.

Ted had the air of melancholy satisfaction I'd spotted on the faces of boys at school as they saw you turn up beside them on the headmaster's carpet. It read "Caught you, too, did he?" Once we were seated, Fred dowsed the lights and the real ordeal began. Arthur's early home movies of the Great Barrier Reef. The projector breaking down was the high point. When it did, the relief was tangible.

In spite of it all, my liking for Arthur continued. We met his protégés, Western and Eastern, and their families: People who had only the most generous praise for his kindness. Self-absorbed he might be, and a teetotaller, but impeccably a gent, through and through.

He was absolutely unshakeable (and why not?) in his faith in his own visions. After all, SatCom was by no means his only accurate prediction. He retained a faith in the power of reason and science to cure our ills. At one point, when the Tamil Tigers emerged on the Sri Lanka political scene, I asked if he wasn't worried. He assured me that it was all a misunderstanding and that the Tigers, who subsequently became expert terrorists, were basically sound chaps who'd soon give up their wild ideas. His view of our world, rather like P.G.Wodehouse's (whom he resembled physically) didn't include much room for the Four Horsemen galloping through his rhododendrons. His preferred future was extremely Wellsian, full of brainy people sitting about in togas swapping theorems.

And he was unflappably The Ego. After we watched the preview of 2001, Aldiss, Ballard and I all admitted it had left us a bit cold in the visionary department. He took our poor response with his usual amused forgiveness reserved for lesser mortals and told us how many millions the movie had already made in America.

Around that time, I was able to introduce Arthur to William Burroughs. Everyone invited to my party expected the master of optimistic hard sf and the master of satirical inner space to get on about as well as Attila the Hun and Pope Leo. In fact, they spent the entire evening deep in animated conversation, pausing only to sip their OJ and complain about the rock and roll music on the hi-fi. At the end of the evening both were warm in their gratitude for the introduction.

I scarcely read a word of his, apart from a few classic short stories, though I came to publish him occasionally in New Worlds, and he knew I was broadly unfamiliar with his work. He understood this to be my loss. And, as he became a massive best-seller, partly because of 2001, but perhaps even more because of his TV series investigating the paranormal, he didn't change. He would still turn up in the pub to show us brochures for his latest ventures and mention casually all the famous people who admired him, including Rupert Murdoch and Richard M. Nixon, showing us 10x8 glossies of himself with the world's movers and shakers. He still understood that we would rather watch his home movies than enjoy a drunken evening playing with rockets whose only technical secrets lay in the length of their blue touch paper. But, I have to admit, I became much warier of accepting his 'party' invitations.

Angus Wilson once returned from Sri Lanka exasperatingly describing Arthur as the most egocentric person he had ever met. Yet somehow, in spite of everything, Arthur remained a beloved friend for whom I retain only the fondest memories. He was a sweet-natured optimist in a world of grief. I'm really going to miss him.

Michael Moorcock was the editor of New Worlds magazine. He has written hundreds of books and is the recipient of the Guardian Fiction Prize, the Nebula, the World Fantasy Award and many others. In 2008, The Times newspaper named Moorcock in their list of "The 50 greatest British writers since 1945".

Arthur C. Clarke

by Ben Bova

When I was in my early twenties I worked as a technical editor for the Martin Aircraft Company on Project Vanguard, which everyone thought would put the first artificial satellite into orbit. That was, of course, before Soviet Russia launched Sputnik.

This was in 1956; I was a struggling neophyte of a science fiction writer. Arthur C. Clarke was already a giant in the field. He came to the Martin plant, outside Baltimore, Maryland, to do a few days of research for a book he was writing. I was thrilled to think that I would meet one of the world's foremost science fiction writers. I was even more delighted when I was asked to show Arthur around the project and set up interviews for him with our top engineers.

For several days I acted as Arthur's escort through every nook and cranny of the Vanguard operation. I remember driving him back to his hotel in Baltimore through a fog so thick I could barely see the hood ornament on my Chevrolet. Arthur was completely at ease, telling me about *real* pea soup fogs in merrie old England.

When I drove him to the airport for his departure, I did something so gauche that I still blush to think of it. For years I had been struggling with a science fiction novel. As Arthur left my car for his plane, I shoved my shoebox full of manuscript into his arms and asked him to read it and "tell me what's wrong with it."

That dear man took the shoebox all the way back to his home in Ceylon (as Sri Lanka was called then), read the manuscript and sent me a detailed letter analyzing the novel and giving me enough encouragement to make me go on with my writing. I owe my career to Arthur. He was the kindest of men.

Ben Bova was editor of Analog and Omni magazines. He has written dozens of books and has won six Hugo awards. He is the President Emeritus of the National Space Society and was President of the Science Fiction Writers of America.

The Sentinel

by Keir Dullea

When I was about 12 years old I became a science-fiction fan. I subscribed to all the science fiction magazines of the time such as Galaxy, Astounding, Fantasy and Science-fiction and so on. I read yearly collections of science fiction short stories. When the 2001 script was sent to me in 1965 something was terribly familiar when I read it. Then it hit me. Years before I had read Arthur C Clarke's "The Sentinel" and I then realized that Kubrick had based his script on that story. What a coincidence!

Cut to the moon landing in 1969. I was making a film in the Bahamas when one of the networks contacted me about doing an interview while they were waiting for the astronauts to emerge from their ship, which if you may remember was many hours after their landing. Just as the interview was winding up, someone ran into the room and yelled "come into the control room, they're coming out!". They seated me in front of a monitor and when I looked to my right there was Arthur C Clarke sitting next to me. As Neil Armstrong emerged I happened to glance over to Arthur and I saw tears in his eyes. It was very moving.

Keir Dullea is a Golden Globe winning actor who played the character David Bowman in the motion picture 2001: A Space Odyssey and 2010: The Year We Make Contact. He has appeared in more than two dozen movies and more than 40 television shows. He has also appeared in several Broadway stage productions.

Arthur C. Clarke

by Robert J. Sawyer

Sir Arthur was my all-time favorite science-fiction writer: no one has ever done a better job of engendering that sense of wonder that good science fiction is supposed to bring about: that feeling of transcendence, of realizing just how big and incredible the universe really is—that special thrill that comes from beholding what Canadian poet Archibald Lampman called "the wide awe and wonder of the night."

In the science-fiction field, there are three major awards for the best novel of the year:

- the Hugo, which is the international people's choice award, voted on by the attendees of the annual World Science Fiction Convention;

- the Nebula, which is the field's academy award, voted on by the active members of the Science Fiction and Fantasy Writers of America;

- and the John W. Campbell Memorial Award, named for the great editor of the SF magazine originally called *Astounding Stories* and now known as *Analog*; the Campbell is the field's principal juried award.

Now, as it happens, one of my books has won the Hugo, another the Nebula, and a third the Campbell Memorial. But in the whole history of science fiction, only three books have ever taken all three of those awards—SF's true triple crown. Those books are Frederik Pohl's *Gateway*, Joe Haldeman's *Forever Peace*, and Arthur C. Clarke's *Rendezvous with Rama*.

What makes that book so special? Well, in fairness, it's *not* the characters—those were never Clarke's main concern; he was never particularly interested, on a literary level, in individual human beings—but he was endlessly fascinated by humanity as a whole, and its place in this great vast universe of ours. It's a tricky thing to make the reader feel both humbled and exhilarated at the same time, but Sir Arthur managed it brilliantly in *Rendezvous with Rama*.

I think Clarke was the greatest science-fiction writer of the 20th century. The novel widely regarded as his masterpiece is *Childhood's End*. More than half a century after it was first published, it's still relevant and timely—for it deals, in part, with a world on the verge of nuclear disaster, something that, sadly, once again seems plausible.

In fact, it's fascinating to compare this early work by Clarke with his final one, *The Last Theorem*, his collaboration with Fred Pohl, published shortly after Sir Arthur's death in 2008. In both *Childhood's End* and *The Last Theorem*, a solution is found to the problem of some portion of humanity wanting to blow the rest of us up. But in *Childhood's End*, that solution comes from aliens, whereas in *The Last Theorem*, it's we humans that devise our own answer. And maybe that's the real end of childhood, for science-fiction: moving beyond the fervent hope that beings from the stars will uplift us from our current state, to realizing that we ourselves will have to solve our own problems.

As I said, *Childhood's End* is probably Clarke's best novel—but when he passed away, all the obituaries mentioned *2001: A Space Odyssey* instead. Now, most accounts say that the screenplay of *2001* was inspired by Clarke's short story "The Sentinel," and that's true as far as it goes: just as in the opening of *2001*, human astronauts find an artefact on the moon in "The Sentinel," and the artefact signals its builders that humanity has now left Earth.

But *2001* is really a story of transcendence, of rebirth, of the next stage in human evolution, and of encounters with almost godlike aliens—and the seeds for all of that are not in "The Sentinel," but rather in Clarke's masterwork, the brilliant and heartbreaking *Childhood's End*.

It's been five years since Arthur C. Clarke slipped through the Stargate, and now we've lost his brother—and biggest fan—Fred Clarke, too. But Arthur's legacy is certain; he will be read with pleasure far into the future.

Robert J. Sawyer is the author of dozens of award-winning novels. He is a multi-recipient of the Hugo Award. His novel Flash Forward *was made into an ABC television series. His latest novel is* Red Planet Blues. *Visit his website at sfwriter.com.*

Chapter IV - The Clarke Legacy

An interview with Fred Clarke

by Mark Stewart

There are certain names which will always be associated with the BIS: Gatland, Cleaver and Parry amongst others. But perhaps one name more than any other can still send a frisson through the Society, recalling as it does both the heyday of the British Interplanetary Society (BIS) and the achievements of its most famous member. That name is Clarke.

The first person who comes to mind when you mention that name is the man who was twice Chairman of the BIS and who will always have a special standing in the Society's history. But there is another member of the Clarke family who is equally deserving of recognition. The tireless hard work of Fred Clarke, both as a distinguished member of the BIS, and as a passionate supporter and champion of his older brother's achievements, demands recognition and perhaps re-evaluation. With this in mind, we travelled to Suffolk, to meet with Fred – who was about to celebrate his 90th birthday – and his daughter Dianne. We were the second BIS contingent to visit Fred in the space of a few weeks. This time the delegation from the BIS consisted of Mark Stewart, Colin Philp and Kelvin Long.

Fred displays many of the qualities associated with his brother; there was the same quick wit and mischievous sense of humour, and the same West Country burr in the voice. There was also the same sense of fortitude and determination in the face of physical adversity and the vicissitudes of ageing. I had always admired Arthur's ability to live life on his own terms, and it quickly transpired that this was a trait shared by his brother. Fred was facing two hospital operations in the week following our visit but that prospect did nothing to dampen his lively spirits. Fred has been a staunch supporter of the Society for many years, often attending events celebrating Arthur's work and life. These contributions continued to the end of his life, with Fred having recently met with the BIS History Action Group, to help with research into a book which the group is preparing on Val Cleaver. Of Val, Fred commented: "He was everyone's uncle. I remember Val saying to me once, when he was working for Rolls-Royce, that he'd had an offer to join a firm in the States: *they'll build me a factory, give me my own staff to work with, my wages will be a helluva lot higher and I won't have to pay so much tax.* He said: *I've turned it down, silly fool that I am. I'm British and I want to work for Britain.*"

Fred was concerned to learn of the Society's current difficulties, as indeed Patrick Moore had been during a recent similar visit by the BIS. And like Patrick, with whom he is close friends, Fred is keen to help the Society through this challenging phase in its history, and ensure that it continues as a well-respected voice in the world of astronautics. If the BIS were to close, Fred felt "*this would be a very great shame; it would have saddened Arthur immensely.*"

On a happier note, talk quickly turned to a project that has been in the planning stages for several decades. For many years there has been talk of a possible *Clarke Centre* in Arthur's hometown of Minehead – a museum containing books, awards, artefacts and memorabilia associated with Arthur's many accomplishments – and this is still very much a possibility. The Minehead Centre is clearly a long cherished project for Fred and something he would dearly love to see happen, as would many members of the BIS. Fred told us the Society could help by contributing back issues of *Spaceflight* and *JBIS*; the journal in particular came in for high praise from our host, who described it as "*a damn good magazine.*"

Fred grew up with his sister (Mary) and his two brothers (Arthur and Michael) on the family farm Ballifants in Somerset in the 1920s and 1930s. A highly engaging account of those days can be found in Fred's book *Four Heads in the Air*. It was at Ballifants where Arthur undertook his first scientific experiments, constructing a radio set and telescope, and where he accumulated an impressive collection of science fiction magazines. "*I kept a few of them,*" Fred told us. "*They used to come over on the ships from*

America before the War, and were used as ballast. Tuppence each they cost. Woolworths used to buy them up and our local Woolworths was opposite Richard Huish School, where Arthur and I went. Arthur used to whip out during the lunch-hour and pop over to Woolworths. He'd go to the big table at the back of the shop where the magazines were; a lot of them were in bits and pieces. Arthur would go through them, the science fiction ones, until he could get a complete story."

During our visit we discovered that the young Arthur Clarke had often helped other children with their homework during the bus ride into school each day. "The school masters often wondered why so many of the questions had the exact same answers!"

We asked Fred if he had a favourite amongst all the stories Arthur had written and his reply created something of an enigma, referring as it did to a collection of stories written for a younger audience; a Clarke fan amongst the BIS membership may be able to help identify this mysterious volume (which is definitely not *Dolphin Island*, the one book which we do know that Arthur wrote for younger readers.)

Arthur's legacy encompasses the worlds of both science fact and science fiction. It includes the concept of the geosynchronous communications satellite and winning – at least once - every major award as a science fiction writer. Of all these achievements, Fred felt that Arthur would be remembered most for his work with Stanley Kubrick on *2001: A Space Odyssey*. "*When someone suggested to Stanley that Arthur would be a good choice to write 2001, Stanley said: "What – that chap who lives in the jungle?" Arthur was already writing for Time-Life when "2001" came up. Stanley and Arthur got on so well and were always trying to outdo each other with gimmicks, with the latest technology. Stanley was one of those people who always seemed to be sucking information out of you; he never missed a trick or an important detail; he even spotted a scratch in the famous monolith the day it was delivered to the film set. You could see right through the block of Perspex so the carpenter made up a wooden box, painted it jet-black and that's what you see in the film!*" We were somewhat distraught to learn that this priceless film artefact - one of the most iconic objects in the history of the cinema

- ended up being broken down and made into pencil lighters after the movie had been completed.

Fred added: "*I had a phone call late one night and it was Stanley asking to speak to Arthur urgently. So I woke Arthur up, made him a cup of tea to get him on his feet. Anyway, Arthur and Stanley were on the phone for quite some time. It transpired that Kubrick had realised that in the year 2001 they wouldn't be using rockets to launch ships into space; he decided they'd be using electric propulsion, which would require a complete redesign of the movie. Arthur knew the film was already behind schedule – the timetable had gone haywire – and MGM was toying with the idea of calling the production off; so Arthur had to persuade Stanley to leave things as they were. And luckily Kubrick did."*

Reminiscences then turned to the sequel to *2001*. Fred can still recall the London premiere of *2010: The Year We Make Contact* in 1984: "*Princess Diana and Prince Charles were both there, though what they made of the film, I was never quite sure!*"

The eldest Clarke brother was Sri Lanka's most famous ex-pat for many years, achieving the highest civil honour of Sri Lankabhimanya, in 2005. We learnt that the Sri Lankan climate had never appealed to Fred, though he had visited Arthur there "*half a dozen times.*" Fred informed us: "*They have a lovely bust of Arthur in the Galle Face Hotel in Colombo, Sri Lanka, though I don't think they'll let us have it for Minehead!*"

Fred was a published author in his own right, a writer/publisher who helped set-up the Clarke family's *Rocket Publishing Co,* as well as an experienced – albeit now retired – heating engineer. In addition to *Four Heads in the Air*, Fred also published an account of his exploits in the Burma campaign in World War 2, under the title *The Road to Spiderpore*. Fred was a member of the 81st West Africa Division. "They were lovely lads I served with; full of fun despite the danger we were in."

At the time of our interview Fred was working on two new books *A Life Remembered*, and a novel about "*a space cruiser searching for new worlds.*"

He was also hopeful that Arthur's publishers might print a special centenary edition of *Indian Ocean Treasure* (first published in 1972) to mark the 100th anniversary of Arthur's birth in 2017.

As with Patrick Moore, Fred could clearly recall the seminal lecture given to the Society in 1948 by Olaf Stapledon, entitled *Interplanetary Man*. Fred revealed that *Last and First Men* – Stapledon's epic novel about the evolution of Mankind measured over cosmic time spans – was one of the most significant influences on his brother.

Arthur once famously said, in the pages of *Spaceflight*, that we shouldn't be disappointed with the progress that has been made since the Apollo Moon landings, and we wondered if this was a sentiment which Fred shared. It was obviously a question which he'd considered before: "*Look what's happening in Japan with the radiation problem,*" he told us sadly. "*We're getting into a state where we're tearing the world to bits, creating an atmosphere we can hardly breathe. Sooner or later we're going to have to find somewhere else to live. Arthur always said the future was on Mars rather than on the Moon.*"

Our hour and a half with our host passed very quickly indeed and for much of that time we felt that Arthur was there in the room with us, an almost physical presence brought to life by his brother's energy and enthusiasm. Before we left, Kelvin presented Fred with one of the Society badges as a small token of our appreciation for his support of the BIS. In talking to Fred Clarke we knew we had captured some highly precious memories for the Society's own *Clarkives*.

We left Fred, and the quiet environs of Suffolk, feeling that the 200 mile round trip had been more than worthwhile, and with a sense of great privilege at having met the other Clarke, a man whose charm and intelligence were equal to that of his brother. Kelvin concluded the encounter by observing: "*Now I can say I have met both Clarke brothers!*" In a way, we all had during that very special meeting.

Arthur and Fred: life-long friends and brothers, location unknown

Arthur in his beloved Sri Lanka

Chapter V - Tales from Taprobane

An Interview with Nalaka Gunawardene

On a freezing day in December of last year, with snow and ice affecting much of the country, a little bit of Sri Lanka came to the BIS in the very welcome form of Nalaka Gunawardene, a long standing associate of Sir Arthur C. Clarke. Nalaka had graciously accepted an invitation to attend the Society's annual Christmas Get Together. The theme for the 2010 event was Sir Arthur's visionary contributions to spaceflight in both fact and fiction. While at the BIS, Nalaka shared his memories of working with Sir Arthur in the following interview.

When and how did you first meet Sir Arthur?

Growing up in Sri Lanka we always knew and respected Sir Arthur as our most celebrated foreign resident. I'm trying to recall when I first met him: I think it was as a schoolboy, initially interested in whales and dolphins, believe it or not! I was doing some research on this subject, and we had pretty limited access to information in those days before the internet (in the early to mid-eighties); so I went to his office-cum-residence and he very kindly let me refer to his library. He had a very good collection because he too was interested in whales and dolphins, amongst many other things. So that's how I first met him. He was just being kind to an eager and enthusiastic schoolboy. Then when I had just finished high school, the government had recently started an institute that they named in honour of Arthur C. Clarke – an institute for promoting science and technology. They organised a programme called "Science for Youth" for the brightest high school leavers. They selected 25-30 of us on a competitive basis from around the country, and we were given weekend sessions on the frontiers of knowledge at that time, for example, on energy, robotics, computers and astronomy. At the end of that programme,

Sir Arthur came and gave us the certificates so that was the first time we actually properly met.

Do you still have that certificate?

I do.

That must be quite a cherished memento.

Yes. And those who were in that initial "Science for Youth" programme, some of them have gone on to become professional scientists and astronomers. The Computer Society of Sri Lanka actually traces its origins to that programme, and the Young Astronomers' Association of Sri Lanka was also conceived there.

What did Arthur most want to be remembered for?

That's easy. I worked on the 90th birthday reflections video with him. If you remember, in that video he said he'd done a number of things in his time – been a promoter of space exploration, an avid amateur astronomer, a populariser of science, etc. – but more than anything else he said he wanted to be remembered as a writer, who hopefully stretched the imagination of his readers. I think Arthur would be happy with the news that the *Guardian* newspaper here in the UK has just voted *2001: A Space Odyssey* the greatest science fiction movie of all time. So Arthur's impact is still being felt, certainly as a writer.

What was Arthur like to work with? He's been described as a gentle and soft-spoken person but with a fairly wicked sense of humour at times. How would you describe him?

It was always interesting. He had the curiosity of a child, of a ten year old – and I say that advisedly being the father of a teenager too! He was always curious about everything under the Sun: he always asked lots of questions, and there were no dumb questions in his book. And as his staff, we were equally encouraged to be inquisitive, and to ask more questions than we might actually be able to answer. On a practical day-to-day level, he was an easy-going man who had a great sense of humour. He used to say that there is nothing in this world that we can't really make fun of – and he actually proved the point by writing a funny short story about the end of the world! Once, when he was in his 80s, he was very amused to read his own obituary printed (in all seriousness) by an aviation magazine in the US. He made fun of everything. The way I sum it up is that he never took himself too seriously – but that he took his writing and his other work very seriously. And that made him an amiable, easy-going person to work with.

That strikes me as a good philosophy for a teacher to have.

Let me add this: not everyone found this quality either charming or appealing. Some people actually found it rather disappointing that he wasn't this crusty intellectual that they somehow expected him to be! I was once told – before I started working with Sir Arthur – about a visiting British author who'd come to see Arthur. He'd spent an evening with Arthur and gone away completely disappointed because the man he expected to see was not the one who greeted him and entertained him. Apparently Arthur C. Clarke in person was not sufficiently profound for this visitor. (Of course, Sir Arthur's own favourite definition of an intellectual was *"one who had been educated beyond his intelligence"*… a category he was careful not to fall into.)

What was Arthur working on when he died? Was there a particular project that he was trying to complete?

He completed *The Last Theorem* literally in the nick of time. The process of writing the *The Last Theorem* started sometime in mid 2003 and progressed in fits and starts until early 2005. By that time, the entire story had been plotted out, detailed notes made, and the first few chapters actually written. Then he had a case of prolonged writer's block which prevented him from completing it as a solo project. As a result, a co-author was found by 2006, and this collaboration with American science fiction author Frederik Pohl took the project forward. They worked from their respective locations (in Colombo, Sri Lanka, and Palatine, Illinois, USA) and were in regular contact swapping ideas and draft manuscripts. The two authors did not get to meet in person during this collaboration, but they were old friends who had known each other for decades and that helped. The manuscript was finally signed-off with Sir Arthur's approval just a few days before his death. He was hugely relieved that day – it was the 15th March 2008 – when I typed the final e-mail to his co-author, as well as to his agents in London and New York, saying that he was very happy with the way the book has turned out. The whole process – with these two octogenarians writing the novel on two opposite sides of the planet, each with their own health problems – had its own set of challenges. There were other projects that he wished to see happen but, for commercial reasons more than anything else, those did not materialise. For example, he was keen to bring out illustrated editions of some of his early books on the oceans. He also wanted to do more television work but the agents and publishers didn't find these proposals commercially viable at the time.

Arthur was very accessible to his fans and he seems to have welcomed anyone who arrived at his home to pay their respects. This seems very different from some modern authors who are very stand-offish and difficult to contact other than by their agents. That seems to have been one of his most endearing traits that he would allow people to knock at the door of his home and get a book signed. Is that your impression too?

Yes, and the reason he gave was simple. He felt that if anyone had spent money buying a book of his, then the least he could do was to oblige with an autograph and a photo opportunity. So he readily agreed to do these, which practice was sustained right up to the very end. Even when he was in and out of hospital, sometimes ignoring medical advice, he would still spend short periods of time chatting with eager fans visiting from different parts of the world. Some people had waited for years or decades for those few moments: he received many fans from Eastern Europe in the last few years of his life. He knew that people in those countries were only able to travel overseas after the Iron Curtain fell.

And every serious letter and e-mail was answered. That was a good part of our work as his staff. We first had to do a preliminary sorting of the crackpot communications from the serious ones. Every correspondent who seemed eager and genuine received a reply. It may have taken a few days or weeks, depending on how much we had to cope with, but our instructions from Sir Arthur were that every letter should have a reply within a reasonable period of time. There was a small team of us providing this support. He had a professional secretary, Dottie, who used to deal with most of the routine correspondence. Then there was Rohan de Silva who handled all the electronics, computers and videos, and in the latter years, also matters related to the internet. My own role was to provide information research, more scientific communications, and liaise with different media companies local and global.

A job to die for!

Well, I didn't always please everyone because we had to be selective. But we made sure every request was carefully reviewed and discussed with the two agents and, where relevant, with the Arthur C. Clarke Foundation anchored in the US. I was Sir Arthur's principal liaison for the Foundation, as well as two universities where he was chancellor up to 2002 (University of Moratuwa in Sri Lanka, and International Space University).

What was his reaction to the 2004 tsunami? I've read that it affected him on a personal level because it wiped out his diving school but it was also a catastrophe that affected his adopted home in Sri Lanka. How did he respond to that?

I was there in the hours and days that followed the tsunami. Initially none of us realised the extent of the damage. It took a while – a day or two – for all the damage to be assessed and for us to realise how devastating the impact had been. Sir Arthur's first concern, and that of his business partner Hector Ekanayake, was the safety of their staff who were based in Hikkaduwa, a hundred kilometres south of Colombo where the tsunami's impact was much greater. (Colombo was spared the impact because it was on the other side of the island, so the waves didn't really have the force to do any damage there.) We were relieved to find out that the Underwater Safaris staff had managed to save their lives but only just: all the equipment and the diving school were lost. And then the news reports came in about how widespread the damage was; two thirds of the coastline was affected; 40,000 people were dead or missing; one million out of a total population of 20 million displaced. All in a matter of a few hours – Sir Arthur was very, very affected by all this – he was shocked and saddened. Once he recovered from that initial shock, he issued an appeal to all his friends and fans worldwide to help Sri Lanka in this humanitarian disaster, and the tragedy that was still unfolding.

Has the island now more or less recovered?

I would say that the recovery has to a great extent now been made – but it took a lot of time and effort for that to happen. Looking back, I think one other casualty of that tsunami was "The Last Theorem." The impact of the tsunami had such an emotional effect on Sir Arthur. He had been writing "The Last Theorem" as his solo project on and off for over two years; but after the tsunami happened, he just couldn't get started again. Nobody said it at that time in so many words – not even Arthur – but I now consider that project a lesser known casualty of the tsunami. If not for the tsunami, maybe we would have had a solo novel. Instead, as I said earlier, it became a collaboration with a co-author.

He wrote with other authors such as Gentry Lee.

Yes, those collaborations had happened years earlier. The first collaborations were, in fact, with Mike Wilson – the talented English diver, writer and film maker who also settled down in Ceylon at the same time. After some years, they pursued very divergent paths, but always kept in touch. In the 1980s and 1990s, Sir Arthur collaborated with Gentry Lee, as well as with other writers such as Mike McQuay, Mike Kube-McDowell and Stephen Baxter. At that time he was doing some solo projects and meanwhile also participating in collaborations. But he started off *The Last Theorem* very much as a solo project, and wanted to complete it that way – but found that after a while, it wasn't happening.

Without wishing to be disrespectful to those other writers many of his fans might feel that his solo efforts were always the best; that seemed to be the pure Arthur Clarke coming through without any distillation. That was very much the case with for example "3001: The Final Odyssey" which he wrote by himself. That was to me pure Clarke and it was a lovely novel.

Yes. I have my own views on the different collaborations. My personal preference is for the Stephen Baxter collaborations. I believe those books come closest to the style and rhythm of Arthur C. Clarke solo works of fiction. Stephen is a Fellow of the BIS; he'll be doing a talk here in February 2011. The BIS motto is *"From Imagination to Realty"* and Stephen's talk is an inversion of that motto: *"From Reality to Imagination"* because we now seem to be going full circle.

Did Arthur regret that the space elevator never became a reality in his lifetime? With the Space Shuttle being mothballed, it would seem that we need a cheap means of reaching Earth orbit now more than ever.

Sir Arthur used to say that the first space elevator would be built thirty to forty years after everyone stops laughing about it. Alas, that date didn't arrive soon enough for him. But he was very happy during the last few years of his life to see the idea being taken seriously by NASA and ESA, with funded plans being developed. Twenty five years after writing about it in *The Fountains of Paradise* he welcomed the serious interest from the agencies that may eventually build and use it.

Amongst the many books that Arthur wrote did he have a particular favourite? Perhaps "2001: A Space Odyssey," which he wrote at the same time as the movie was being made?

He did have a personal favourite but that wasn't *2001* or *Childhood's End*. It was *The Songs of Distant Earth*, which was first published in 1986, a solo effort. But he used to say that it's very hard for a writer to choose a personal favourite from amongst his own work; it's a bit like a parent being asked to choose a favourite child from among the brood. He didn't really explain his choice; he just said that he liked that one slightly more than the rest.

What do you think Arthur would have made of the decision to phase out the Space Shuttle? Would he have felt it was premature?

At the time the Space Shuttle started flying in the 1980s, I remember him calling it just a transitory phase in space travel; that while it was a great improvement in efficiency over the Saturn Vs and the other early non-reusable rockets, he always felt that the Shuttle wasn't the answer, that it was too inefficient, too costly and as it turned out, also a bit too hazardous. He had no grand illusions about the Space Shuttle; he felt it was a necessary phase. Looking back, I suppose he would have celebrated the end of that particular phase, had there been something to immediately succeed the Shuttle. He was very supportive of the Ansari X Prize and personally endorsed it. He keenly followed its progress and cheered when it was won by SpaceShipOne of Burt Rutan.

Did Arthur often talk about the BIS? You've mentioned the phrase "Space cadets" and that's how he used to describe himself and his early colleagues back in the 1930s. Certainly a lot of his non-fiction refers to the BIS and his role in helping to set it up before the Second World War intervened; and then acting as President on two occasions in the post war years. Did he often reflect on those times?

Yes, he did. He had the Society's bound journals on his bookshelves sitting close to him. He often talked about the Society and his time as a member and one time Chairman. He was always interested in the current developments in the BIS. *Spaceflight* magazine would arrive every month in the post, and he would go through it eagerly cover to cover. The BIS was very much Sir Arthur's spiritual home and it always stayed with him. He had the fondest of memories about his time at the BIS. He always promoted it whenever he could through his writing, television appearances and public speaking. He used to tell visitors from space agencies of the US, Russia, Europe, India and other nations that humanity's journey to space started as a private enterprise by a couple of pioneering rocket societies and the BIS!

If Arthur had patented the idea of the communications satellite he'd have been the richest man on the planet; his fortune would have been incalculable. I think Wireless World paid him something like £15 for the article in which he described the concept of a global communications network made possible by geosynchronous satellites. Did he ever regret not patenting the idea?

That was a question he was asked many times, and he always said he had no such regrets. He added that patents are not worth the legal trouble they come with! And he felt that he had all of the fun and none of the responsibility by being the godfather of the communications satellite, while the engineers who built and launched the pioneering comsats took many risks both technologically and financially. He said he'd made a modest living as a writer and that he was perfectly happy about having lost a billion dollars in his spare time! I see it as one of the greatest gifts to humanity that he didn't sell off the idea, especially when you think about how it's changed the whole world.

What did he most enjoy about living in Sri Lanka?

His short answer was that it allowed him to avoid forty British winters! The long answer took a few books to explain (including *The Reefs of Taprobane, The Coast of Cora* and *The Treasure of the Great Reef*). It was a combination of the tropical climate, the geographical location, the marine environment, the people and the rich cultural heritage. He said there are more beautiful countries, for example, in the Pacific that has very little culture; there are also countries with lots of culture but very harsh living conditions. Sri Lanka seems to have got the proportions just right in a small enough country. He found the island - as an outdoors man, as a diver and explorer of the land and the sea – to be an appealing place. That's why he originally went there, to dive and explore the seas around Sri Lanka.

How did post polio syndrome affect him? Although Arthur was in a wheel chair for many years it doesn't seem to have defeated him at all, he seems to have remained quite active; you've said that he was writing right up till the end of his life. Did he find the initial diagnosis quite a blow?

Actually the initial diagnosis was more drastic. When he found some difficulty with his mobility, and noticed a weakening of his leg muscles, he originally came to the UK. It was in 1986, and the British medical specialists diagnosed him as having amyotrophic lateral sclerosis or Lou Gehrig's disease, which was progressive and terminal; they gave him about three years to live. However, both Sir Arthur and Hector {a friend of Clarke's} refused to accept that diagnosis. Later, he went over to the US and the medical specialists at the Johns Hopkins Hospital made a second diagnosis, which was post polio syndrome. At that time post polio was only beginning to be understood by the medical profession. So Arthur was one of the first and better known cases. The doctors at the Johns Hopkins Hospital said that with enough care and physiotherapy, he should be able to lead a productive life; and certainly they removed the 'death sentence' he'd been given. He went on to live another 20 years, and was highly productive in that entire period: four solo novels, several nonfiction books and dozens of essays, speeches and television productions. Post polio was slowly taking control of his body. He'd had polio as an adult when he was in his 50s, and then made a complete recovery; he had a slight limp but to all other appearances he had recovered. But the illness came back in his seventies, progressively making it difficult for him to move around and eventually confined him to a wheelchair during the last few years.

He was such an optimist that he said being confined to a wheelchair was not such a bad thing for a writer; he could stay in one place and do a good deal of writing and imagining. Around this time, he started speaking out about the rights of mobility-challenged people, the need for better access for those using wheelchairs, especially in Sri Lanka where that thinking had not emerged until quite recently. He turned his disability into a personal crusade on behalf of everyone who faced such challenges in their everyday life.

Thank you Nalaka for braving the British mid-winter and giving us some wonderful insights into Sir Arthur's life. It's been an absolute pleasure to meet you and thank you for your comprehensive replies.

It's a pleasure. All I have really been is a fly on the wall. When I said this to someone who's a respected scientist, and a great Arthur Clarke fan, he said: "Yes, but what a wall -- and what a privileged fly!" I think that sums up the enormous privilege that I've had and I've been very happy to share some of that with you. Thank you for this opportunity.

(This interview was conducted at the Headquarters of The British Interplanetary Society in London and published in the society's newsletter "Odyssey", May 2011).

Colin Philp, Nalaka Gunawardene and Mark Stewart,
British Interplanetary Society Headquarters

Rendezvous with Arthur

by Michael Lennick

For those of us lucky enough to be kids or young adults in the middle years of the 20th Century, the future was bright and well-defined. As American astronauts and their Soviet counterparts blazed trails towards the moon and beyond, iconic years like 2000 and 2001 flared on the horizon in a compelling mirage – the shiny spot down the road where the future we'd been reading about all our lives would truly kick in. Clues to this exciting new era came from scientist/writers like Wernher von Braun and Willy Ley, but my favorite speculations could be found in the works of Arthur C. Clarke, a brilliant storyteller who wrote like a journalist – as though the utterly-plausible yarns he was spinning had already taken place, and he'd been there to bear witness. Every tale seemed to take you on your own personal tour of the future via that rare emissary who was actually in the know – a guide who not only let you share in the possibilities, but in his spare time was helping to bring them about. (Which was not far from the truth, given his lifelong membership in the British Interplanetary Society and important wartime role in the early deployment of Radar, not to mention a certain 1945 paper describing the geosynchronous communication satellites underpinning so much of today's technology, culture and civilization.) Arthur was first and foremost a wonderful entertainer, but his stories, even the most lighthearted ones, had genuine mass, impacting with the force of a Chesley Bonestell painting (for those of a certain generation) or the first images from an interplanetary probe (for those of another.) His writings filled our heads, dreams and aspirations from childhood on. They're in there still.

Meeting so influential a hero can be more than a little intimidating, but when the opportunity presents itself, you jump. And so it was in the fall of the year 2000, that my wife (and co-producer) Shirley and I journeyed to Sri Lanka in order to interview Arthur C. Clarke for a Discovery Channel documentary on the making of his and Stanley Kubrick's masterpiece, *2001: A Space Odyssey.*

It was a project I'd been dreaming about, one way or another, since the spring of 1968 when our neighborhood grindhouse, the Glendale Theater, finally justified its recent conversion to Cinerama by locking in *2001: A Space Odyssey* for what would be its longest first-release continuous run in the world; nearly three years. I was there for at least 50 Saturday matinees and even the odd evening show – whenever I could goad a friend outfitted with wallet-bearing parents – eighth row back dead center. Thus it felt a bit like a jump-cut thirty-plus years into the future when I found myself convincing the program director of the Canadian Discovery Channel that he should invest in a far costlier ticket – a one-hour special exploring the creation of (and the ideas underlying) Kubrick and Clarke's extraordinary film. Network heads agreed, conditional on an unusually tight deadline. Our next Discovery Channel special, *2001 and Beyond,* would premiere on the fifth of January, 2001 – less than three months away.

So Shirley and I were headed for Sri Lanka - or, with luck, soon would be. There was one other issue to resolve: Stanley Kubrick had died unexpectedly only a few months earlier, making a proper retrospective that much more elusive, while transforming our deal with Discovery into one also conditional on an interview with Arthur C. Clarke, a man I had never met nor corresponded with. Knowing how often those of us who dance in the documentary minefields have to advance reality ever so slightly (some might say lie) in order to get a tricky project rolling, I assured my good friends at Discovery that Sir Arthur was already in the bag.

The great Canadian science-fiction writer (and longtime friend) Robert J. Sawyer was kind enough to provide Arthur's fax number in Sri Lanka. That evening I nervously transmitted one of the most important letters of my career. Arthur responded quickly, providing a mailing address so he could view some of our previous work. A few weeks later we were chatting by email as though we'd known each other for years (I've since been told by those far closer to Arthur than I that this was a common sensation – if you had his attention he would treat you as the most important person on the planet.) Arthur pointed out what we already knew, that he hadn't left his adopted home of Sri Lanka for well over a decade, and had no further plans to do so. If we wanted to interview him on camera we could either do so via satellite, or meet him at his home. Shirley and I immediately opted for the latter, despite Arthur's warnings that this was an election year on his troubled island, and perhaps not the safest time to travel.

Two weeks and thirty-three in-transit hours later we found ourselves in the rear of an ancient, incredibly vulnerable taxicab, hurtling through the teeming cacophony that is downtown Colombo. The single front seat was the purview of our warm and friendly doctor/cabbie Sanjeewa (though he insisted we call him Sammy), who spent most of his time with head twisted towards the rear, filling us in on the local customs, even as several of them flew past us in a 60mph blur.

Arthur C. Clarke was a huge cultural and scientific presence in the capital of his adopted island home – a fact repeatedly verified as Sammy drove us past some of the buildings and institutes named for him. (It was near his statue in the lobby of our hotel, the venerable old Galle Face, that the concierge advised us there'd be no need to tell our cabbie the address – everyone knew where Mr. Arthur lived.)

That first journey to Arthur's mid-city compound took less than twenty minutes, regularly punctuated by soldiers pulling us over to check our ID (their M-16 rifles poking through the rear windows), or the occasional burst of AK-47 fire a block or two over. The first time that happened we asked Sammy what was going on. He leaned back, smiled conspiratorially and whispered, "Campaigning."

Colombo is one of those cities that can rapidly overwhelm you with your own sense of unworldliness, as your tiny, hollow projectile careens past cars, trucks, oxen, those ubiquitous Southern Asian scooter/van combinations called tuk-tuks, and even the occasional elephant carrying a huge teak log in her trunk. Between answering our questions and peppering us with hundreds of his own about life in North America, Sammy would frequently determine that we could be going faster, yanking the wheel hard-left to slam us out into the minimally-defined opposing lanes of traffic. We soon recognized a sort of telepathy in play, as Sammy and the driver of whatever vehicle we were now hurtling towards would calculate the precise moment their game of chicken would turn deadly, deeking back into their respective lanes just before impact. We quickly surrendered to the reality that there was nothing Shirley and I could do from the rear seat to ensure our survival, so our best and only option was to sit back and enjoy the movie unspooling through the windshield, complacent in the surety that neither we nor anyone we knew could drive this course without years of training.

The Clarke estate was a modest yet very beautiful compound whose car park separated two near-identical white houses - one residential, the other containing facilities for a small staff, as well as Arthur's work environment. The walk down the length of his office was one of the longest of my life, past rows upon rows of floor-to-ceiling bookshelves filled with editions of his works in all the many languages they'd appeared. Arthur extended his hand as I approach his desk, and though I struggled to cough up the cleverest remark I or anyone else had ever uttered, I'm afraid what emerged was closer to "I've traveled a very long way for this moment". Arthur immediately tried to put me at ease. "Yes, it's lovely to finally meet you too. I do hope you haven't come all this way to ask me about 2001". As I stood there, trying in vain to draft a response to this unexpected (and unnerving) introduction, he smiled his twinkly smile, adding, "I'm pretty sure it's the only year I'm fated to have to live through twice."

And that was that. We were off on one of the most delightful and awe-inspiring conversations of my life – an experience not unlike finding an unread Arthur C. Clarke novel, only in real time. Arthur suffered from Post-Polio Syndrome and was largely confined to a wheelchair (though he played a truly intimidating game of Ping Pong when braced against the table), so he could only speak on camera for brief intervals. Of necessity our interview stretched out over the better part of a week – which was certainly fine with me. Our topics ranged from technology to spirituality (both of which he supported in their appropriate roles, though he had scant patience for religion), along with a heavy dose of social commentary, all delivered with his trademark wit. I soon learned that he hadn't been kidding at our first meeting. As much as

Arthur admired Kubrick and his work, he still held a few reservations about the final version of the film they'd crafted together, (some of which can be found in his book *The Lost Worlds of 2001*, as well as his subsequent novels *2010: The Second Odyssey, 2061: The Third Odyssey, 3001: The Final Odyssey*, and, of course, his original 1968 novel *2001: A Space Odyssey* – the book we all rushed home to read way back when, if only to discover what the movie was about.) Ever the gentleman, Arthur didn't want to denigrate Kubrick or the film in any way – in fact he strove to avoid the topic. Still, mandates are mandates, especially at the network level, which meant I often found myself asking a related question about a design or description in Arthur's screenplay, whenever the conversation veered in close enough. ("So am I correct in assuming that the nuclear pulse rocket the British Interplanetary Society had contemplated would have come in very handy years later while you and Stanley were evaluating propulsion solutions for your interplanetary spacecraft Discovery....") Arthur always knew exactly where I was going. He would smile, roll his eyes, and then provide the wisest, most thorough answer imaginable. Every one of those comments made it into our film *2001 and Beyond*. All we had to do was cut in right after he finished rolling those sharp, twinkling, incredibly thoughtful eyes.

Arthur and I corresponded for many years thereafter – a distant relationship with a much-beloved acquaintance whose recent passing has left a hole in my life I could not have anticipated. Our libraries may hold his stories, his ideas, but there will be no more forthcoming. And dammit, there was still so much to talk about. As I write this it's mid-April, 2008, and we've just learned from the director of Spaceport America that the good citizens of New Mexico, against all expectations, have overwhelmingly approved a new tax bill that will allow the world's first commercial/civilian spaceport to be born – not too far down the road from the parched desert sands where Robert Goddard launched America, and the world, into the Space Age. The classic dreams Arthur first wrote about in the 1940s are finally coming to pass, just as he always knew they would. What a shame he's not here to see it, let alone take that first ride.

Author's note (2013): Shortly after Arthur C. Clarke died in 2008 I was asked to write this brief tribute. The deadline was tight, with a limit of 2000 words. As a result, this is the only writing I've ever handed off in rough draft form - not due to the time limit so much as the odd discovery that my first draft had somehow managed to clock in at exactly 2001 words.

MICHAEL LENNICK has written and directed documentary series and specials for the Discovery Channel, PBS and others. His work includes the award winning television series "Rocket Science" and "2001 – The Science of Futures Past". His films, articles and books on the on-going story of humanity's adventures in space can be found at www.foolishearthling.com

The Brightest Star

by Helen Sharman

The light, hot breeze ruffled my clothes as I floated in a cloud of euphoria and jet lag down the road to meet Arthur. Colombo was every bit as fantastic as I had imagined: palm trees against a cloudless sky; delicious aromas of Sri Lankan cooking; broad, friendly smiles on the faces of passers-by. Today I was on my way to a book shop, where Arthur had agreed to help publicise my autobiography by doing a joint signing of books: his many stories and my single autobiography. Of course, being one of his local shops, this one was well-stocked with a variety of Arthur's books and our shared publisher had sent a supply of mine for the occasion.

Arthur was keen not to steal the show, though he could so easily have done so, being far the better known of the two of us and obviously held in awe by the store's proprietor. A slow but steady stream of customers came to one or other of us over the next few hours, during which Arthur signed books tirelessly and spoke with people in the most humble of manners. Sometimes Arthur was asked to sign my book, which, although apt as he had kindly written the foreword, seemed incongruous to me, that such a giant in the world of science fiction should have anything to do with a small, young astronaut.

My spaceflight had captured the imagination of Arthur's brother, the lovely Fred Clarke, who had invited me to talk as part of his festival of space in Minehead. It was the beginning of a long relationship, which was to see me visiting Arthur's old school, amongst others, and taking part in a number of events that Fred so energetically organised in the community where he and Arthur had grown up with the rest of their family. It was Fred who had arranged for me to visit Arthur, sorting out everything including an elephant to greet me at the entrance of my hotel in Colombo!

The evening was spent at Arthur's house, sharing thoughts on space travel and future technologies under the gaze of photographs of astronaut-admirers who had visited previously. Arthur's mind was quick and questioning, always with a new idea to mull over whenever one conversation came to an end. Just before dinner we went out onto the flat roof of Arthur's house and viewed Saturn through his powerful telescope, the planet's rings clearly visible against the blackness of surrounding space. The stars were spectacular, too.

But the star that stays brightest in my memory is Arthur himself, someone who probably would never have described himself as such, yet a more dignified and delightful star I cannot imagine. Now, whenever I see Saturn, I always think of that evening with Arthur and his shining example of how humble and kind a great star can be.

Helen Sharman, OBE, was the first British woman in space. She flew to the Mir space station in 1991 and is the author of two books. She is a Fellow of the Royal Society of Chemistry and is currently a lecturer and broadcaster.

Chapter VI - Remembering Arthur

Members of the British Interplanetary Society Reminisce

Martin Fry

I am a Fellow and have been for a long time. In the seventies I worked in the aerospace industry and then moved on, but continued my interest right through the eighties. In the early nineties I set-up my own business and subsequently had no more time, so I've been a "sleeping Fellow" ever since.

During my active time I was a member of council for a number of years, but I can't remember exact dates. The point of all this is that in 1982, I chaired the *Space 82* BIS Conference in Brighton. I'm afraid I have no recollection of the theme, but what I do remember was interviewing Arthur via a satellite link. He was in Sri Lanka and it was very early days for that sort of communication. It was fixed up free by the BT of that era. I remember being told 'you can speak with him from x minutes and y seconds past the hour and the link would be open for 5 minutes and z seconds. His image appeared on a big screen.

I'm afraid I have no recollection of what our conversation was about, but there may be some record in the BIS archive. I know the interview was well received by the delegates.

David A. Hardy

In 1952, having been guided to a scientific rather than an artistic career, I began work as a lab technician at what was then the College of Technology in Birmingham (now part of the University of Birmingham at Aston). I had just become a member of the BIS – I'm now a Fellow – and had heard that there was a Midlands Branch. There being no internet in those days I searched everywhere, such as the libraries and CAB during my lunch hours. Finally, I discovered that it met... at the College of Technology! The speaker at one of the very first meetings I attended was Arthur C. Clarke, and indeed I produced a poster advertising it. And of course I got to meet the great man (I had recently bought his *Interplanetary Flight* and *Exploration of Space,* and was of course influenced by artist R.A. Smith, who I also met at a later meeting). I remember especially how Arthur showed a slide of himself on the Moon, with the spacemen of *Destination Moon.* I used this superimposition technique myself years later for the inside jacket of *Challenge of the Stars,* with me sketching on Titan with Patrick Moore looking on (much easier today with digital techniques!)

I met Arthur several times after this, and he possessed two of my paintings. A photo of us was taken at the launch of said *Challenge of the Stars*, a book for which Arthur also wrote the Foreword – as he did for the sequel, *Futures/50 Years in Space* in 2004. I also provided the cover art for *The Snows of Olympus,* and he used my work in other books and his lectures. I gave an illustrated talk at his 75th in Minehead in 1992 (an age I have now reached myself).

David A. Hardy and Arthur C. Clarke

Mat Irvine

In earlier years he was still travelling a lot and while the Clarkes (well, Mother Clarke and Fred) still lived in 88 Nightingale Road in Wood Green, and I was still based

Arthur and Mat Irvine

in that area, I would see him, though more in passing, when visiting Fred. He came to the various Space Exhibitions which ASH (our local Astro Society Fred started) put on in the early 1970s.

Later, I do remember well the famous occasion when he was the surprise mystery guest at the SF Convention at the Radisson at Heathrow, when I chaired the meeting; then of course the *This is Your Life* programme. Plus I do have a copy of "my" script of *A Fall of Moondust* signed by him. The last time I actually saw him was at the BFI for the showing of the re-mastered *2001* - which of course was after Stanley died.

Bert Lewis

I am sure many BIS members were or are very keen SF enthusiasts. It played a large part in stimulating my interest and belief in the possibilities of spaceflight, starting with the sale of American SF magazines imported into the UK as ballast on cargo-ships and sold on market stalls for 3d (three pence) and with the "quarterlies" at 6d (sixpence). Although some of the critics of space possibilities were very scathing, a lot of the stories were eventually seen to be only too accurate in their forecast. And why not, some of the authors were actually scientists in their own right.

About that time I found a correspondent in a young man, Arthur Clarke, a student at Taunton Grammar School, and actually met him during a touring holiday in Devon, a tousled-haired youth all worked up over science fiction. Then, in 1955 he came to Preston to give a lecture on space flight. My wife and I were able to put him up during his stay. The thing I remembered most clearly was the difficulty in getting him down from the library to a meal. My enthusiasm for science fiction is still very strong, now having a nice collection of what I consider to be the "cream" of the genre, approaching the 700 mark.

Kelvin F. Long

Around the year 1999 or 2000, I and some friends had just finished our end of year degree exams. We decided that a good way to celebrate was a visit to the London Science Museum, in particular the space section. Whilst walking around I noticed an elderly man sitting in a wheel chair, but somehow filled with the vigour of youth. He was surrounded by perhaps four other people. The man was pointing up to an exhibit that read *Arthur C. Clarke invented the communications satellite.* As I looked at the exhibit, then the hand and back to the face of the man, I realised

this was Arthur C. Clarke getting a guided tour. I was very excited and immediately told the others. One of my friends went up to the party and asked if we could briefly meet Arthur and have our photograph taken, I would never have been so forward as to interrupt him in that way. All the same, I was glad he did. Arthur agreed and we huddled around the Apollo 10 re-entry capsule which was

Kelvin F. Long and Arthur C. Clarke, London Science Museum (1999)

on loan from the US Smithsonian Institute. I recall little of what we spoke about, as the meeting was quite exciting for us young students, although I do recall 'science fiction' being mentioned and Arthur referring to us as *"his fan club"*. He was very kind and shook all our hands and quite frankly made our day.

At the time of the Science Museum encounter I was only vaguely aware of Arthur's work, particularly *2001: A Space Odyssey*. I hadn't read much of his writing back then, although I had admired him for years, particularly with his 'Mysterious World' television series which I very much enjoyed. When I was young I had a wonderful book by him called *Of Time & Stars* which is a collection of short stories. I still have the book and have read it many times. The book resonated with me and even then I knew there was something important in this work. After the Science Museum meeting I did get interested in Arthur to a much greater extent, particularly after joining the British Interplanetary Society and discovering the important role he played in the early days. I subsequently read almost everything he has ever written on the subject of space exploration, both science writing and science fiction, although I still find the occasional gem I have not read. My favourite works by Arthur are *A Fall of Moondust*, the entire collection of the 'Odyssey' books, *Rendezvous with Rama, The Songs of Distant Earth* and *Childhood's End*. However, my favourite book of Arthur's which I really loved was *The City & The Stars* and it had an almost Stapledonian feel to it. Reading the story filled me with happiness and the dance of life. As I went on to work in the aerospace industry and begin to think about how I should best direct my energies towards space exploration, I began to see that my own aspirations were manifested in the writing of Arthur C. Clarke. Hence the goals of my life became dedicated to his optimistic self-fulfilling prophecy and it is with this motivation in mind that I founded *Project Icarus*, the successor design study to the BIS *Project Daedalus*. Rejuvenating the research field of interstellar flight became an important objective for me personally.

I have subsequently read the excellent biography *Odyssey* by Neil McAleer, as well as many other accounts of his life and the person that he was. I also read the book *88 Gray's Inn Road* by his friend Bill Temple, which contained highly amusing accounts of Arthur stealing the sugar from the local cafe and the shenanigans of the early BIS meetings. Reading the accounts of what sort of person he was as a young man made me warm to him as a person, and I regret never having got to know him in a personal capacity, other than that one encounter at the science museum. I think Arthur was a very kind person, giving to others, compassionate and with the heart of an innocent child. And like a child is how he viewed our species, on the shore of something great and as I believe Newton once said *"with the ocean of knowledge before us."* He had a global perspective on our species that others lacked and exhibited a boundless optimism for our ability to solve all problems, given time and the will. He believed in the potential of the human spirit to rise to unprecedented levels of advancement. He thought deeply about what possibilities await our future, both good and bad, thoughts which others dare not go to. This is I think what gave him his visionary quality and allowed him to see the future where others failed. He also had a paradoxical approach to his writing, emphasising hard science fiction and the importance of science, yet willing to speculate on things which others would view as bordering on the metaphysical.

He often spoke about biological humans not being the end point of evolution but merely an important part of an even more advanced destiny, fully evolved artificial intelligence – Clarke called this *"homo electronicus"*. This always struck me as odd, because if this was true then by creating this future, we could be working towards our own demise; the end of the biological human. But, I realised this is not necessarily true and Arthur viewed us as being a mere stepping stone to something greater than ourselves, an important role for our species.

When Arthur passed away, I first saw the announcement on *Sky News* and was saddened by it although I had been expecting it. He had made a wonderful broadcast on *You Tube* only months before on the occasion of his 90th birthday, which essentially carried the message, *"let me lay quiet in the night, seek not other than to question, the books I leave behind"*. This was a very powerful message which I took on board. At a recent BIS lecture in 2011, the writer Stephen Baxter said that he thinks in time Clarke would be re-examined as a writer. I think this is quite true and people have barely glimpsed some of the implications for the words he put to paper. He saw more than the rest of us, and once we catch up, his legacy as a brilliant man and a good human being will be secured for history.

Sir Patrick Moore

He was a great visionary, a brilliant science fiction writer and a great forecaster. He foresaw communications satellites, a nationwide network of computers, interplanetary travel; he said there would be a man on the Moon by 1970, while I said 1980 – and he was right. The space elevator: not one of Arthur's better ideas! A

Sir Patrick Moore with Fred Clarke

great man, a great visionary, he was right more often than he was wrong; most of his ideas have come to pass and the rest almost certainly will.

The BIS was founded in 1933. I joined in 1934; at the time I was twelve years old. Arthur Clarke was also a member and he came up to me and shook my hand at my first meeting; he was seventeen and we struck up an immediate friendship that lasted the rest of our lives.

The BIS didn't have a regular H/Q in those days. Many of the first meetings were held at Claxton Hall. The Society closed down completely during the war. Other early members included: Ken Gatland, Len Carter, Val Cleaver, Archibald Low, Phil Cleator (the first BIS President) and Ralph Smith. The BIS never carried out many experiments because of the Explosives Act of 1875!

Ray Ward

I was interested in space from an early age, mainly through an interest in science fiction, and I read Arthur's fiction and non-fiction avidly. Eventually I wrote to him in Sri Lanka and he sent his standard reply with manuscript annotations including advice to contact the BIS, which I joined in 1971.

I then lived in Sheffield and therefore couldn't get to BIS meetings, but one I was determined not to miss was when Arthur came to London, soon after I joined, and addressed a meeting at the Royal Commonwealth Society. I arranged to go with a friend and then travel back to my friend's home not far from London.

Clarke was fascinating and I still recall some of the things he said, like the money saved by weather satellites alone, by preventing death and destruction, could pay for any conceivable space programme. I also recall the great roar of laughter when he said (and I recall his exact words): "If I hear any more about Teflon non-stick frying pans I shall throw up!" This, of course, referred to the myth that polytetrafluoroethylene (PTFE), better known by its best-known trade name, Teflon, came out of the space programme; it was in fact first produced in the 1930s. Thousands of new and improved products have come out of space research, but the only one most people have heard of is wrong; and still, nearly 40 years later, we find people (including some who should know better) saying "Did we need to send people to the Moon to get non-stick pans?"!

I got Arthur's autograph and took a flash photograph, and recall his remark: "Oh, my sun-burned retinas!" I then sent him a copy. It showed a hand pointing into the picture, and he replied thanking me and making some comment that it looked as if he was being fingered by an unidentified informant!

I joined Mensa in 1973 when Isaac Asimov was an International Vice-President. The following year he was persuaded to come to Britain on the *QE2* (he wouldn't fly), and the organisers found Arthur was going to be in London at the same time and invited him to introduce Asimov. This too I couldn't miss, so off I went to London. There was a reception at the Savage Club where I found myself in the same room as Clarke and Asimov! Asimov spoke at the Royal Commonwealth Society, introduced by Clarke (I have a cassette tape of the event). In *Odyssey*, Neil McAleer's biography of Arthur, there is a photograph of Arthur introducing Asimov, with some fuzzy blobs in the foreground, and I'm certain one of them is the back of my head, because I was sitting in more or less exactly that spot! There was also a packed, rather riotous gathering at a science fiction fans' pub in Hatton Garden, attended by Asimov and Clarke, with people spilling out onto the pavement, autographs being collected, etc. The Clarke-Asimov Treaty, concluded in the back of a taxi in Washington, DC, long before, was mentioned. Under its terms, Clarke was the best science fiction writer and the second-best science writer in the world, and Asimov was the best science writer in the world and the second-best science fiction writer. So Asimov said that whenever Clarke is asked who the best science writer was he always said Asimov and whenever he was asked who the best science fiction writer was he always said – at which point I shouted: "*Bob Heinlein!*"

1979 saw the first annual Mensa at Cambridge gathering (which is still going), at which Clarke was one of the speakers. He arrived at Trinity College with his brother Fred. I reminded him of our previous meetings and told him I'd brought my copies of first editions of several of his novels and asked if he would sign them, and he said he would. When he arrived at the lecture theatre he saw me with the heap of his books, sat beside me and signed them all. And his lecture was brilliant! I also have a first edition of the American edition of *The Exploration of Space*, which I bought for $1.25 in a second-hand bookshop on Hollywood Boulevard in Los Angeles in 1973 and which Arthur signed either at the 1974 or 1979 events – I'm not now sure which.

I met Arthur at least once more, in London (at the now-defunct

Commonwealth Institute, I think; I can't remember exactly when), when he spoke about the treasure discovered while diving off Sri Lanka. He brought along a mass of silver coins which had solidified into a single lump in the shape of the bag, which had, of course, long ago rotted away. Members of the audience were allowed (under the watchful gaze of a security man) to try lifting it, and very heavy it was too.

At the British Interplanetary Society's Space '93 conference in Hastings a sound and vision link with Arthur in Sri Lanka was set up via a mobile BT satellite dish parked outside, and several people, including Patrick Moore, Buzz Aldrin and me, conversed with him. The BIS issued a VHS video of the event, which I have, though only Arthur is seen, the others being in sound only.

I had long before written to Buckingham Palace urging that Arthur be honoured, preferably by a knighthood, so when I heard of his knighthood I contacted him (by fax, I think) and said I was glad to see the Queen took my advice, however belatedly! He was kind enough to telephone me personally at home to thank me - alas, I wasn't in, but he left a message.

If one 20th century Briton is still remembered in 500 years I think it'll be Arthur, and I'm delighted and honoured to have met him and had other contacts with him. A few more details come to mind:

Arthur's theme at our first meeting was of course the benefits of space, and he showed a clip from a film he had made about predicting a flood in Sri Lanka.

The 1974 visit was no doubt helped by the fact that one of the leading figures in Mensa, Victor Serebriakoff, who rescued Mensa and built it up when it was threatened with extinction, was a friend of Arthur's. He said he tried to persuade Arthur to join Mensa, but he said he wasn't the joining kind. Victor used to hold monthly "think-ins" in London at which a speaker (Mensan or non-Mensan) would talk for a while and then matters would be opened up to general discussion, with Victor always scrupulous about letting everyone who wished to contribute do so. I went to nearly all when I lived in London, but after one that I missed I learned to my great frustration that Arthur was there!

David Baker

I remember very well the time when Stanley Kubrick's people came to the Marshall Space Flight Centre and used all the future NASA planning drawings and concepts that appeared as the space vehicles in *2001: A Space Odyssey*.

The novel was written by the two of them and one evening in America, Arthur suggested that they should decide to whom primary authorship should go. It was over some fish meal the two of them were enjoying and napkins doubled as note pads! Kubrick was the one to say that he felt the written word was strongest and he respected Arthur Clarke so much that he wanted Arthur to have credit for the book if he could take the film - and that was that. Wernher von Braun got personally involved as well, couldn't be kept out of it.

Arthur mentioned to Stanley that he should make friends with von Braun as the latter was well in with Walt Disney from the *Conquest of Space days*. So the trio of major players was set. Then we got around with the Stanley Kubrick folks and showed them all the future stuff that was coming up. This was while I was tasked with working with Raymond Loewy Snaith on Skylab interior design so I got to show Kubrick's people a glimpse of the future we were planning at NASA. Loewy of course was a design icon, having done the Coke bottle and leading US cars of the '50s. He was tasked with doing the interior colours for Skylab (I still have the drawings we used with him, bearing his pencil notes) and von Braun thought it would help push and popularise what was then emerging in our imagination, and planning, as a future littered with shuttlecraft, space stations and missions to Mars.

Just about this time the initial concepts of a shuttlecraft were being given flesh through the Integral Launch and Re-entry Vehicle (ILRV) studies that really started in 1966 and peaked with the integrated plan of September 1969 that formalised all this exciting stuff. I saw Arthur and Kubrick together and they really hit it off but we were suddenly all like schoolboys again, revelling in that proverbial candy store. Never saw either of them again but NASA, the world,

America, and all of us space cadets were now living in a very different place.

For me the brilliance of Arthur Clarke was that he kept the dream alive beyond the point where there was any real hope of doing anything about it. We were all living on borrowed time and even scarcer money; the NASA budget was tumbling through the floor, Vietnam was turning very nasty, race riots were tearing up the streets – but I didn't live within any of that, thanks to Arthur and the work he did with Stanley. Beyond the point where the dream could be kept real, Arthur created a new place where we could all go and transcend the realities of the moment for a glimpse, ever so tiny, into a future none of us will ever see but which we know will one day come about. And it is a very special person indeed that can create a universe such as that, one in which we can all live, in hope and anticipation, that our genes – rendered immortal through our children – will one day form the flesh and bones that will walk the red dusty plains of Mars, or swoop low across the Galilean Moons.

Along with *Journey into Space* and *Dan Dare* before it, Arthur's visionary tales provided the oxygen for our aspirations. I'm still breathing that!

Fred Ordway, Deke Slayton, Arthur Clarke, Alfred Alibrando, Stanley Kubrick and George Mueller. The three NASA people visited the 2001 set (dubbed NASA East) at Borehamwood on 25th September 1965. Ordway came straight from the tennis court for the meeting.

Chapter VII - Treading the Sands of Mars

Arthur's Work in Retrospect

The City and the Stars, reviewed by Kelvin F. Long

This book was first published in 1956 and is based on an original short story entitled *Against the Fall of Night*. Before I read the book several years ago, I had just finished reading the twin pillars of Olaf Stapledon's literary career: *Starmaker* and *Last and First Men*. I knew that Stapledon had been a big influence on Clarke and this was prominent throughout the pages of *The City and the Stars*.

The story is set initially in the apparently Utopian city of Diaspar, a billion years in the future. The citizens of Diaspar are immortal; the humans are created by machines and people can die and be reborn from the computer, which stores their life's memories. To maintain population control, the computer chooses which citizens to awake from their virtual death in order to live another lifespan in Diaspar. In the story, Clarke proposes a definition of the ideal machine: that *"no machine may contain any moving parts"*.

The central character – Alvin – is different from his contemporaries because this is his first life and in some ways he is responsible for the renewal of human civilization to come. But Alvin has a passion, to get outside of the city and explore, an almost infectious obsession that drives his every action. Eventually, he is helped by what can only be described as a deliberate and mischievous anomaly in the computer program (called Khedron) that shows him the way.

There is a fundamental paradox in the story. The city of Diaspar is a perfect place, but the world outside is not. After a long period of galactic war the city of Diaspar is the last resting place of humanity, protected from any would-be invaders by a large domed shield. Humanity was once a star-faring species but has been forced to adopt an insular existence. Diaspar is also a form of dystopia, offering its inhabitants all they could ever want including immortality, but inhibiting their freedom to explore the world outside.

Outside the city is the human settlement of Lys, an apparently technologically less advanced place with no interest in space travel, consisting of mortal people who have perfected mental telepathy. In Lys, Alvin meets a companion called Hilvar and together they explore the planet. Eventually they meet an ancient extraterrestrial creature and his fellow robot that are loyal to their masters – The Great Ones.

Their journey leads them to the discovery of a spaceship and they are able to leave Earth and travel to meet a powerful but child-like being of pure intellect called Vanamonde, who can travel through space instantaneously. They establish a telepathic communication with the being. From this encounter they learn the truth of what happened to the rest of the human race and the terrible deeds of the insane being known as The Mad Mind, a form of mentality, which had been imprisoned inside a Black Star.

Like much of Clarke's writing, this story contains a powerful blend of credible science fiction and large ideas which border on the metaphysical. Clarke maintains a perfect balance between these two limits and demonstrates, as he does with many of his other books, that he is a corking good writer. The City and the Stars is one my favourite science fiction novels by Clarke. I left the book wanting to know more, about where Alvin travelled to next.

(Originally Published Issue 3, May 2011, BIS Newsletter Odyssey)

The Sands of Mars, reviewed by John Silvester

To see how it would stand up as a science fiction novel today, I decided that on holiday this year I would re-read *The Sands of Mars*, which I had not looked at since my childhood years in the 1950s. This was Arthur C. Clarke's first novel. It was published in 1951, when the author became Chairman of the British Interplanetary Society for the second time, and just a few years before the launch of Sputnik 1 heralded the arrival of the space age in 1957.

The central character Gibson is a writer, and the story revolves around his trip to Mars aboard the first purpose-built passenger space ship *Ares*. He finds Mars to be a benign place, and with some limited plant and animal life. After his Martian plane crashes he goes on to discover a small colony of harmless ruminating animals. The author stops short of calling them the Martians, thus leaving open the prospect that other more intelligent creatures could perhaps exist somewhere else on the planet. It is a gentle story, which the author carefully sets against the background of what was known and inferred about Mars at that period of time: a world without craters, and with a much warmer and thicker atmosphere than we now know to be the case.

This would have seemed credible in the 1950s. Unfortunately the relentless onslaught of data from robotic spacecraft has dated the story. The result is that it can now only be read as a period piece, as one would treat the writings of Jules Verne and H.G. Wells. Originating at a time when Britain had started down the long road of colonial withdrawal, it contains - perhaps not surprisingly - a hint of the problems of Empire, for example, the reference to the huge cost of maintaining a Mars colony.

There are also numerous instances where the author demonstrates his legendary foresight; there are two in particular that are worth mentioning. A process to release oxygen from the soil represents an interesting early concept of terraforming. However, the idea of turning Phobos into a second Sun now comes across as rather fantastic in a novel of this nature. It may have seemed less so in an age when nuclear processes were in their infancy and the possibilities looked endless.

Clarke does not describe the physical appearance of the characters, and there is a certain hollowness about them as a result. Nevertheless this deliberate style does not detract from the book's atmosphere. It still grips as a story and retains a vitality that makes you want to continue to the end, a tribute to Arthur C. Clarke's abilities as a writer.

(Originally Published Issue 8, October 2011, BIS Newsletter Odyssey)

The Sands of Mars, reviewed by Adam Crowl

Arthur C. Clarke's *The Sands of Mars* recounts the adventures of a younger Clarke, thinly disguised as Martin Gibson, science fiction novelist, as he travels to Mars. Gibson achieved his first taste of fame with his best-selling novel, *Martian Dust* (1976), written while recovering from a nervous breakdown in his college years. In Gibson's later fiction he moved away from the Red Planet, but his early fame has come back to haunt him with a writing assignment he couldn't refuse. Ostensibly contracted to promote emigration to the Red Planet to Earth's best and brightest, by writing up his own journey and sojourn there, his journalistic instincts soon detect that the new Martians are covering something up. Something big, cryptically called "Project Dawn".

Gibson uncovers an even greater secret, which fifteen years of human exploration of Mars had failed to discover, animal life. He also rediscovers a son he had almost forgotten he had fathered, from the relationship that precipitated that fateful nervous breakdown over twenty years before. Thus through the course of his Martian adventure his life comes full circle and he finds himself anew as a new Martian.

Clarke's interplanetary trilogy from the early 1950s – *Prelude to Space*, *Islands in the Sky* and *The Sands of Mars* – draw upon the technical discussions of the British Interplanetary Society in the 1930s and 40s, as well as his own discovery of the value of geosynchronous orbit space stations in 1945. He very optimistically, for the time, predicted Moon landings by 1975 and Mars landings shortly after, with settlement of Mars, Venus and the Moon well underway by the 1990s, when *The Sands of Mars* is set (c.1995.) Thousands of people occupy multiple space stations around the Earth, in the cities on the Moon, and colonies on the Inner Planets, in Clarke's vision of the dawn of the 21st Century. Of course, in our alternative history, neither Mars nor Venus has proven as hospitable as hoped, and microelectronics replaced the need for permanent crews of technicians to replace vacuum tubes on space stations.

That vision of another history inspired *2001: A Space Odyssey*, but by the year of that film's release, 1968, the dream of manned bases across the Inner Planets was becoming an increasingly hard sell, and something we still don't have firm plans for nearly fifty years later. What made the Clarkean vision possible – nuclear propulsion – still remains experimental hardware. Yet what made his vision *necessary*, the spread of humanity to other planets, remains with us still. Modern day versions of the Interplanetary Trilogy are yet to be written, but they're needed today even more than the originals were nearly sixty years ago.

Childhood's End, reviewed by Gregory L. Matloff

When I found this book again after a search in a used bookstore, it was reconnecting with an old friend. Published by Harcourt, Brace and World in an arrangement with Ballantine Books, the frontispiece of the edition I purchased has a copyright attributed to Arthur C. Clarke dated 1953.

As a young boy just before the dawn of the Space Age, I first came across *Childhood's End* in my local library. It had a profound effect and pointed me in the direction of my eventual career.

How did Clarke present so many prophetic concepts in one 220-page novel? His predictions of geopolitics were accurate with a description of the Moon Race between the US and USSR. Of course in this novel, humanity's burgeoning space programs are truncated by the arrival of our extraterrestrial educators and masters, the Overlords.

In 1953 Clarke predicted the development of a holographic technology, since one huge Overlord ship suspended above New York City projected duplicate images of itself above many other locations. I remember thirsting as a youth for more information regarding the antigravity device and projection technology of the Overlords.

Clarke's description of interstellar Overlord technology obviously affected many other readers. In Carl Sagan's *Cosmic Connection* (Anchor-Doubleday, 1973), a chapter entitled *The Night Freight to the Stars* speculates on the spectacular appearance of a starship accelerating up to light speed. Clearly, Sagan was affected by the observations of an Overlord ship in flight by a major human character in *Childhood's End*.

Far more profound than Clarke's technological speculations is his consideration of possible future directions of the evolution of humanity and other technological species in the Milky Way galaxy and beyond. Clarke clearly was a pantheist in his spiritual beliefs, as indicated by his treatment of consciousness. Such paranormal phenomena as remote viewing and projections backward in time play a role in this novel. His beautiful and touching consideration of the evolution of the final generation of material humans towards the "Star Child" phase in this novel led to the cinematic adventures of astronaut David Bowman at the conclusion of Stanley Kubrick's *2001: A Space Odyssey*. In this manner, he predicts the research to come in the field of Quantum Consciousness.

Clarke demonstrates the belief that humanity's final destiny might be of a non-material nature. The non-material Overmind that ultimately absorbs humanity (and the Earth) actually controls the Overlords. Although the reader envies the technology of the Overlords early in the book, he finishes by pitying them. They are obviously stuck in the material state while the races they encounter can be educated to move beyond the material plane. I wonder if Clarke was proposing this as a solution to Fermi's Paradox (where is everyone?) in an era decades before mathematicians and computer scientists would speculate about the "singularity" (when computers overtake the human brain) and existence in a non-material virtual world.

Another philosophical (or perhaps psychological) aspect of *Childhood's End* is Clarke's description of the physical appearance of the benevolent Overlords. Perhaps foreknowledge of their satanic appearance and how their arrival would end the material phase of humanity gives rise to the concept of the Devil?

As well as its technological, philosophical and theological musings, this novel is an excellent read. The description of how one adult human community chooses to self-destruct after witnessing the rapid advancement of their children beyond the human realm never fails to move me.

Childhood's End should be required reading for anyone interested in interstellar travel, contact with extraterrestrials, the future of humanity or the evolution of mind in the universe. It has already affected the work of countless scholars and artists. And for a book published in 1953, it is still surprisingly topical.

Rendezvous with Rama, reviewed by Paul McAuley

Rendezvous With Rama (1973), written at the height of his fame, winner of just about every award in the science-fiction field, is Arthur C. Clarke's third novel about First Contact. In the first, *Childhood's End*, devilish aliens arrive on Earth to uplift the children of humanity and supervise their fusion with a cosmic overmind; in the second, *2001: A Space Odyssey*, aliens represented by enigmatic monoliths gift the ancestors of *Homo sapiens* with the capability for abstract reasoning, and thousands of years later signpost the way to a Star Gate that transmits an astronaut to a place where he is transformed and given the key to the next stage in the evolution of human intelligence. *Rendezvous With Rama* takes an entirely different approach. Its theme is not cosmic awakening, but the vastness of the universe and its indifference to human endeavour.

In the first chapter, set in 2077, a relatively small meteor smacks into Northern Italy, 'destroying in a few flaming moments the labour of centuries,' and killing six hundred thousand people. To prevent similar cosmic accidents, the people of Earth create Project SPACEGUARD (a nice example of Clarke's prescience: a decade after the novel was published, the name of his fictional project was borrowed for a NASA study on how to protect Earth from a serious meteor strike). Fifty years later, SPACEGUARD spots something hurtling through the Solar System on a sun-grazing trajectory: an alien starship, named Rama by its human discoverers. Only one spaceship is capable of matching Rama's velocity. The race is on to explore it and attempt to make contact with its crew before it passes too close to the Sun.

Rendezvous With Rama is by no means a perfect novel. Despite the problems of having one wife on Mars and another on Earth, the leader of the exploratory team, Commander Norton, is oddly bloodless, and the rest of his crew are only lightly sketched, and include rather too many people who just happen to possess the right kind of expertise required to solve the problem at hand. References to the voyages of Captain Cook and the discovery of Tutankhamen's tomb contribute to a quaint, Boy's Own Adventure feel that's reminiscent of Clarke's early stories, in which astronauts fry sausages in their Moon buggies and alien treasures are dispatched to the British Museum rather than the Smithsonian. Ideas are interjected via the talking heads of the Rama Committee, which appears to operate out of a Pall Mall club. The notion of using genetically altered monkeys to carry out the routine tasks aboard a spaceship finds no foothold in the story.

None of this much matters. Clarke's alien starship is a potent and iconic artefact. There's a nice passage describing the rescue of a stranded explorer, and an attempt to inject some drama when the aggressive colonists of Mercury decide to park a precautionary H-Bomb next to Rama; but most of the novel's power comes from carefully calibrated revelations about a pharaonic project that embodies the vast effort required to traverse interstellar distances without violating Einsteinian physics, and investigation of its strange landscapes, described with Clarke's characteristically lucid precision. Rama's huge cylinder is hollow, with what appear to be cities on its inner surface, a world-girdling circular sea dividing it in half, and a cluster of huge, mysterious spires at the far end. At first it appears to be derelict, but as the heat of the Sun penetrates its thick hull the human explorers witness a brief spring as the lights come on, the Circular Sea melts, and biomechanical robots (biots) appear and busy themselves with mysterious tasks.

But despite the best efforts of the explorers, Rama remains enigmatic, and impervious to human intervention. They fail to have any meaningful interaction with the biots, and learn almost nothing about the nature and purpose of the ship's builders, who 'would probably never even know that the human race existed'. The Solar System is merely a way point on an interstellar voyage that has already lasted longer than the span of human civilisation, with a destination that is nowhere in the galaxy; instead it is 'aimed squarely at the Greater Magellanic Cloud, and the lonely gulfs beyond the Milky Way.'

Much science fiction – especially much American science-fiction – is driven by bumptious optimism. The universe is our oyster; all we need to do is figure out the right tools to crack it open. *Rendezvous With Rama* is a necessary corrective: a grand adventure, and a fine and rigorously thought-through lesson in humility.

Earthlight, reviewed by Adam Crowl

With some later embarrassment Arthur C. Clarke wrote one of the most compelling accounts of an interplanetary battle scene in his *Earthlight*, both as a novella (1950) and a novel (1955). The tale focuses on the efforts of an ill-equipped spy, Bertram Sadler, forensic accountant, sent to the great Observatory in the Mare Imbrium, to uncover the source of a flow of sensitive information to the interplanetary colonies from there. The novella version of the story Clarke sets in c.2015, some 40 years after the first Moon landing, with the conflict chiefly over supplies of uranium. Five years later, for the novel, he pushed it back to 2175, with Mars and Venus extensively settled and terraformed. Rare heavy elements, not power metals, are now the cause of the conflict, but much of the story remains the same.

Arthur C. Clarke's interplanetary stories and novels from the early 1950s drew upon the technical discussions of the British Interplanetary Society in the 1930s and 40s, as well as his own discovery of the value of geosynchronous orbit space stations in 1945. He very optimistically, for the time, predicted Moon landings by 1975 and Mars landings shortly after, with settlement of Mars, Venus and the Moon well underway by the 1990s. Thousands of people would be occupying multiple space stations around the Earth, cities on the Moon and colonies on the Inner Planets, in Clarke's vision of the dawn of the 21st Century. In the novella version of *Earthlight* this leads to Venus declaring independence at the turn of the millennium, with Mars and bases on Outer Planet Moons following soon after. In the novel the break with Earth is more gradual, growing from Earth's discontent with the success of its colonies.

Most of the novella focuses on the climactic battle-scene, when ships of the Interplanetary Federation attack Earth's "Fortress" on the Moon. Both sides have new technologies – the Federation has inertialess drives, giving the ships extreme manoeuvrability, while Earth's Fortress is equipped with a highly effective particle weapon ("polarons" in the novella, liquid metal in the novel) and a force-field. The battle scene is down-played unsuccessfully in the novel, as the rest becomes a kind of travelogue of life on the Moon, seen through the eyes of Sadler. He is the Clarkean Outsider, a proxy for the reader, who is then introduced to the new idea of life on the Moon (or Mars or in orbit or in the build up to the first Moon-landing, as in the other Interplanetary novels of the 1950s.)

Unfortunately for Clarke's sense of embarrassment in writing the battle-scene, it is truly the climax of both the novella and the novel. The antagonists end their hostilities with no civilian casualties and a dramatic space rescue of the crew of one of the Federation ships. Clarke's endless optimism and true humanism comes to the fore here, as the two sides driven to violence are then more ready to reach a new accord, as if embarrassed by doing something so uncivilised as actually fighting. In later novels he foresaw the end of hostilities between the Superpowers in a similarly civilised fashion, such as in the wake of the detonation of Jupiter in *2010*. History hasn't been kind to Clarke's prediction of a near-term human future amongst the planets, but his vision still inspires and his hope for a peaceful end to mankind's many conflicts is very relevant today.

2001: A Space Odyssey, reviewed by Mark Stewart

"Its origin and purpose still a total mystery."

Almost fifty years after Clarke and Kubrick joined forces to create the "proverbial good science fiction movie," *2001: A Space Odyssey* remains the ultimate celluloid enigma. There's an apocryphal story in which a studio executive, at the end of a private screening of the film, scrawls a single question across the cover of his movie programme: *What does it all mean?* The answer of course depends on who's watching the movie, or reading the book. Kubrick called *"Cut!"* on the final scene in *2001* over four decades ago, yet this film – originally entitled *How the Solar System was Won* - still inspires, challenges and baffles like no other movie. I don't think Clarke or Kubrick fully understood their creation; like a sculptor or painter they conjured from their combined imaginations a work of art – and it *is* a work of art by any definition - that demands attention and appraisal, provoking a reaction at an emotional, almost intuitive level.

The geometrically shaped monolith is a clever metaphor for something that few science fiction writers have convincingly described, contact with an advanced extra-terrestrial culture. There are no ludicrous prosthetics in *2001*, no masked humanoids – so obviously men in suits – capering unconvincingly through a preposterous storyline. Actors, of course, portray the simulated colony of apes with which the movie begins. But this subterfuge is easily overlooked – a slight of hand comparable to the one achieved by Pierre Boulle in his own monkey tale – and the movie remains the closest contact many of us will ever have with an alien intelligence.

For all its mathematical and rectilinear precision the monolith looks utterly alien, terrifying both the apes that encounter it in the primeval dawn and the astronauts who, millennia later, excavate it on the Moon. In a movie chock-full of lingering images, one that stays in the mind more than most is the image of Heywood Floyd reaching out to touch the surface of the sentinel at the bottom of the pit dug in Tycho Crater. It seemed at the time entirely plausible that Floyd – who surely embodied some of Clarke's own scientific curiosity - would be whisked away to the ends of the universe as soon as his fingertips made contact with the obsidian surface. And in a way that's just what happened, but to Dave Bowman rather than Heywood Floyd. The mysterious hotel room at the end of the universe – in which Bowman travels along an evolutionary trajectory at a dramatically accelerated pace – is nothing more than a way station, a momentary hiatus in a journey that sees mankind elevated to the point where it can manipulate the destiny of stars, an ability which Clarke's literary mentor – Olaf Stapledon – described in his own novels.

That wonderful shot of the gliding spacecraft, the one which replaces the tumbling bone thrown into the air by Moon-Watcher in the biggest fast-forward in movie history, catapults the viewer into a future which we somehow let slip away, and which now seems more unachievable than ever. It's an odd paradox that a movie about the future can now make you feel nostalgic. The movie appeals to *"men of a certain age"* – to coin a phrase used by Stephen Baxter – to men who were kids at the time Neil Armstrong was leaving boot prints in the Sea of Tranquillity; kids who were busy building model rockets they were destined never to fly in adulthood. For those of us who watched the real Dave Bowman's and Frank Poole's as they rode their Saturn Vs into orbit, *2001* was *our* Apollo, our trip off-world, all for the price of a cinema ticket or the cost – quite reasonable back in those days – of a paperback book. The ultimate value-for-money road trip, a highway that extended all the way from the Earth to Jupiter and beyond. And travelling that road changed us all, hopefully lowering our tolerance for the trashier, undemanding end of the chaotic sprawl that is science fiction, past and present. In a genre that sometimes cries out for respectability, *2001* is still a rallying point for anyone interested in serious speculation, and mind bending possibilities; for anyone passionate enough to proclaim: "This is what our genre can do; this is what makes it different; this is what elevates it above the mainstream."

Some elements of the mystery can be pegged down; it's easy to say what certain parts of the movie are about: evolution; exploration; a blue print for the future, which the space agencies have studiously avoided following; First Contact; immortality (who really believed that Hunter, Whitehead and Kaminski, the sleeping hibernauts who expired when HAL turned off their life support equipment, were really dead; much easier to believe that they were still alive as Discovery sped outwards to its mysterious rendezvous, three emissaries of mankind waiting to be roused from their long slumber as soon as they encountered other travellers in the interstellar deep). All of these motifs are present but if ever a movie was more than the sum of its parts it's *2001*. For many critics at the time the psychedelic ending was a trip too far, even for the tail end of the sixties. These days talk of multi-verses, SETI, exoplanets and possible forms of astrobiology are much more common.

Ironically, for a writer who was often criticised for portraying unconvincing human characters, Clarke created a highly humanistic, not to mention spiritual; story, even if that humanity is best and most convincingly expressed through HAL: a computer forced into psychosis by deceitful humans. Who can blame HAL for finding it difficult to understand humans? Which one of us doesn't have that same problem on an almost daily basis and how many wars have their origin in such shortcomings? Perhaps it's HAL that should have gone on to explore the infinite inner dimensions of the monolith rather than Dave Bowman. He might have been able to make more sense of it.

In the end *2001* is whatever you want it to be, depending on how you interpret the almost subliminal ideas it conveys. It's that rare movie where the audience gets to decide what the ending means. And perhaps not just the ending but the entire movie. Long live the enigma.

Growing Up: Childhood Ends, reviewed by Andy Sawyer

No, not a spelling mistake. This is not the 1953 classic. In fact, it's a very rare book indeed, a limited-edition collection of the very earliest surviving writing by Arthur C. Clarke, culled from the pages of his school magazine *The Huish Magazine* by editor David Aronovitz, whose "Portentous Press" published the book in 1996. The copy in front of me was donated to the Science Fiction Foundation by the author's brother, Fred.

Anyone's "school magazine" offerings can be a source of much embarrassment, as I discovered several years after re-reading a short story in which I obviously thought "contretemps" was a cool way of saying " counterpoint". Fortunately, there's nothing of that magnitude here. The contents of *Childhood Ends* are a collection of skits, essays, and the occasional semi-fictional piece which flesh out the picture of Clarke given by his brother in his biographical essay in *Foundation* 41. They are obviously the work of a bright youth with an interest in matters scientific, and already that science-fictional imagination is at work. A series of spoof "letters from Old Boys" is set in increasingly bizarre and exaggerated climates, including "Mt Hiasell" which projects into the stratosphere and allows the author some speculation on space-like conditions and "British Malaria" where the description of intense heat is, as the author suggests, obviously based upon descriptions of other worlds in science fiction magazines. Literary ambitions are already in place. In "The Fate of Fu-Manchu" that wily oriental evil genius comes up against Conan Doyle's Great Detective. Shakespeare's *Julius Caesar* is transposed to New York, where tough-guy gangsters shoot it out.

There's also biographical interest. An affectionate description of Clarke himself is given by one of his schoolmates in a piece in which "Professor Larke" is working on an epoch-making experiment through which "we shall either be transported into the future or onto the Fourth Dimension. You see, my notes got rather muddled..." According to the Professor, the School Organ "could be greatly improved by attaching one of my patent electro-static, super-magnetic, hyper-heterodynic, electronic Wattnottophones". In another piece, (inspired by the 1937 film of Wells's *Things to Come*), a far-future version of the school is visited and "one of the speakers, Klahk 15, is very learned and appears to be instructing the other." Clarke appears again as "Clericus", the name with which many of his pieces are signed, in a mock-Shakespearian play entitled *The Mystic Potion* in which his learning and willingness to share it is sent up:

> When yonder star that's eastward from the pole --
> I mean of course, N. B. G. one-two-seven
> Of spectral type/or thereabouts
> Has moved through forty six point seven degrees
> Our rites commence.

In contrast to this "eccentric professor" image, an unusually serious young Sir Arthur (or perhaps it was his co-writer, R. B. Canaver) laments in a Brendon House report that "We are sorry to say that the House is bottom in the Keenness Competition."

160

This is enjoyable but fannish stuff, which we smile at because this schoolboy with scientific ambitions is now extremely famous for both science and writing while at the same time we wonder how for many other local geniuses appearance in their school magazines was the height of their careers. But later pieces show us a Clarke more recognisably the one we know. "Interviews with Notorieties no. 1", signed with Clarke's familiar fannish pseudonym "Ego" gives us a self-portrait of a Professor with a fascination for setting off space-rockets and a huge collection of "weird-looking magazines" with titles like *Fantastic* and *Science Stories*. This piece, Clarke reminisces, was written after he joined the British Interplanetary Society, as was "Into Space", a more serious article signed "Arthur C. Clarke, Treasurer, British Interplanetary Society", which argues seriously that space travel is no idle fantasy but is simply a question of time, experience and money. Its beginning is recognisably the style of the Clarke we know, in which his argument is based upon a detailed description of the Earth as seen from space, or at least from a balloon in the stratosphere taken in 1935. Both romantic and realistic, it's a sign that we can see the world in a different way. A similar article is entitled "The Greatest Adventure". For untold ages, Clarke says, we have looked up at the stars and speculated about them. Now we are beginning to know what they are. Is it possible that, at last, we could build upon our knowledge of space to *travel* in it?

Although in some ways wildly optimistic (and certainly, as the Clarke of 1996 wryly observes, less based on cold fact than the Clarke of the past recognised) these are closer to the work of the mature writer. The bright 14-year old who contributed the early articles for a readership of schoolmates has become the visionary 19-year old writing to argue a case to a wider audience. Childhood ends.

Included with the book are a number of photographs. One is an often-reproduced image of the teenage Clarke, head bowed in concentration, at work on some electrical apparatus (perhaps to improve the school organ?) But there is also the frontispiece; a two-year-old Clarke with the most glorious head of curls I've seen since – well, since my own childhood photographs – staring to the side, away from the photographer. It's not, perhaps, fanciful to wonder whether he is considering the world before him, not sure what he will do next.

But (we are certain) he will think of something.

(A slightly different version of this was published in Matrix 162 (July/ August 2003), published by the British Science Fiction Association).

Arthur's Guide to the Universe, by Mark Stewart

Where did it all go wrong? We caught the symbolic bone – Clarke's tumbling conundrum – thrown into the air by the clever ape; but, contrary to all expectations, it didn't transport us to the stars, or even to the edge of our own solar system. The baton of technological change passed to a generation that chose to explore *inner* rather than *outer* space, to inhabit the online world, *Space Dreamers* more interested in shooting their virtual opponents than shooting for the stars.

By now, we were supposed to have colonised the Moon and be on our way to the Red Planet, if indeed not already there, having left footprints in *The Sands of Mars.* A ring of space stations, accommodating scientists and tourists alike, circling the planet and clandestine investigations into a strange monolith recently dug up on the Moon: all of this was part of the vision of space – *The Promise of Space* – as foreseen by Clarke and Kubrick back in 1968.

Yet both of Clarke's seminal years, 2001 and 2010, have come and gone, and none of this has come to pass, or is likely to in the foreseeable future. It all seemed very possible at the end of the sixties, so what happened? Even as recently as 1974, with Skylab orbiting the Earth and the Americans and Russians finally about to cooperate on a joint mission, it still seemed as if science fiction could become science fact. But now the decision to abandon Skylab seems to have been a turning point, a fateful choice that involved so much more than allowing America's first space station to burn up on re-entry, comparable perhaps to Lindbergh ditching *The Spirit of St Louis* in mid-flight, or the Wright brothers deciding never to fly the *Kitty Hawk.* The scuppering of Skylab may well have sounded the death knell for America's space-faring ambitions long before the last Shuttle touched down, long before that *Glide Path* to the stars was sealed off.

The decision to develop the Shuttle was correct in principle - a reusable space plane was exactly what Arthur and Stanley foresaw: who can forget the elegant Pan Am spacecraft that took Dr Heywood Floyd to his rendezvous with that iconic space station spiralling majestically to the sound of the *Blue Danube Waltz* – but in practical terms it only ever led to missions in low Earth orbit, and with a few exceptions these flights were never going to capture the public imagination. The lampooning of a shuttle mission in an episode of *The Simpsons* was uncomfortably close to the truth, with the mission controllers describing the tedium of changing a screw in orbit and Homer falling asleep on a couch as he watched.

The glory days of Apollo now seem far away, as mythic and distant as anything in that other more ancient odyssey, buried beneath *A Fall of Moondust*. Future generations will find it hard to believe that we ever walked on the Moon, not because of some crack-pot conspiracy theory but because it was such a colossal achievement done with a less advanced technology than we have now; and because those missions – the very stuff of history - were never followed up. A good analogy would be Columbus sailing to the New World without anyone ever following his route across the Atlantic. Many *Islands in the Sky* await us, if only we have the resolve and the courage to find them. The alternative is a drab and dreary set of *Tales from Planet Earth*, the story of a species which collapsed in upon itself in a perfect ecological storm, an environmental apocalypse created by a run-away human population and a degraded biosphere. Arthur, the patron of an elephant sanctuary on Sri Lanka, would have been appalled to see our continuing mistreatment of the whale and our fellow primates.

Perhaps we are on the brink of a new era in space exploration, led by the private sector. I'd like to think so. But some of the big aerospace companies are still flying paper prototypes, sketching out designs that may never leave the computerised drawing board. And it will only take one accident – for one private space plane to burn up on re-entry, or for one manned capsule to fail on a test flight – for the whole private sector dream to crumble. What's needed perhaps is a global space agency, a United Nations of Space Exploration that can look beyond petty political and national interests; but how likely is that?

The only way back to the Moon may be a new space race. China's plan to land taikonauts on the Moon may finally rouse the American's into action, prompting them to remember their heritage and to look beyond the orbital shallows, out to the Grey Moon and the Red Planet. Think what a three-world system – the Earth, the Moon and Mars – would do for commerce and science, not to mention safeguarding *Homo sapiens* from extinction – from *The Hammer of God* – should a rogue asteroid ever hit *Imperial Earth* again. Should that apocalyptic impact happen at least there would be humans elsewhere in the solar system, but only if we recover the ambition to colonise other worlds. The *Prelude to Space* has gone on long enough; now we need to travel beyond the *Cradle*.

It is hard not to see the shuttle as a dead end, a machine that led the space programme up a blind alley. The heirs of Apollo - of the dozen men who walked on the Moon - got stuck driving an orbital truck. The shuttle is a truly remarkable machine and has achieved wonderful things. But it was only ever meant to be a building block, a stepping stone onto other things. The fact remains that since the flight of Apollo 17, no human being has travelled much further from the Earth than a few hundred nautical miles, and it is difficult to see how this will change in the decades to come. Orbital space is the realm of the satellite and where larger endeavours such as preparing for missions to the Moon and the planets should begin; the embarkation point for journeys *Across the Sea of Stars*.

The true *Coming of the Space Age* is still a dream, the final frontier remains out of reach for most people. But the thing is, we so very nearly got it right: Skylab – America's forgotten programme – showed the way: building a space station out of Apollo components; the same components that could have been used to build a base on the Moon. This is how we might have bridged the gap between imagination and reality. Pete Conrad – surely the most charismatic of the Apollo brotherhood – as the first Moon Base Commander. Why not? And John Young – surely the most laconic – as Chief of the Lunar Shuttle fleet. America has never lacked engineering ingenuity and with the help of the Russians we could have done it. Imagine watching *Earthrise* from the observation dome of a lunar village or city. Getting back from the Moon wouldn't have been a problem either. A surface-based payload launcher is so much easier to build than a space elevator, especially in a low-G environment, and would easily have catapulted capsules and cargos alike back to Earth.

Perhaps what we lack is the Space Age equivalent of Isambard Kingdom Brunel, someone who can attack daunting challenges with relish and achieve the impossible. Someone who can bridge the gulf between the Earth and the Moon the way Brunel spanned the chasm now occupied by the world's first suspension bridge. A visionary engineer unphased by the technical limitations of the age, a man such as Vannevar Morgan, the engineer who built the first space elevator in another one of Clarke's alternative, better futures; we need someone who can rebuild *The Fountains of Paradise* as a 21st century launch site, ambitious architects of the future who can create new ways of getting into space.

The Fall of Night is almost upon us, this closing down of space exploration, but it is still not too late to sail upon *The Wind from the Sun*. In describing future space missions, one of NASA's former Chief Administrators coined a phrase that remains true today: "faster, better, cheaper." And speed may be of the essence: for the chance to do these "big things" is surely waning even as the Earth's population expands and its resources shrink. As Clarke once suggested, it is time to *Reach for Tomorrow*, while that tomorrow is still within our grasp.

Chapter VIII - Old Spaceship

The Spaceship

by Kelvin F. Long

In a century from now, or even a millennium, what will Arthur be remembered for? Will it be for his invention of the communications satellite through his now famous 1945 Wireless World article *Extra-Terrestrial Relays*, or the popularisation of the space elevator through his novel *Fountains of Paradise*? Perhaps it will be for his inspiring role in convincing the world that the vision of manned spaceflight is credible? The American astronomer Carl Sagan has said that Clarke's book *Interplanetary Flight* influenced him as a child.

Clarke also played an important role in motivating research into artificial intelligence, through his *Heuristically* programmed *AL*gorithmic computer (HAL), made famous by the novel *2001: A Space Odyssey* and movie of the same name, directed by Stanley Kubrick. So perhaps this gives us a hint of his legacy – the merging of biology and technology into *Homo electronicus*. Clarke saw *Homo Sapiens* as merely a stepping stone to full-blown AI, as a means of creating more efficient information processing mechanisms. He speculated that rather than flying in spaceships we could then become spaceships.

One of Clarke's nicknames when he was in the Royal Air Force was "Spaceship" and when we were writing this book we gave it the code name "Project Spaceship" for this reason. This is apt, because he played an important role in many actual spacecraft concepts, from the original atomic spacecraft that appeared in his books *Interplanetary Flight* to the 'Ares' of *The Sands of Mars*. The *Ares* was able to reach Mars in around 100 days. He designed interstellar spaceship concepts, such as the *Magellan* in *The Songs of Distant Earth*. This was a vessel containing one million colonists placed in cryonic suspension. It was powered by a "quantum-drive", harnessing the energy of particles that are trapped in the fabric of space itself, a form of space drive. The Magellan travelled at around ten per cent of light speed, and to mitigate particle bombardment by dust grains and interstellar protons, carried a huge frozen water shield at the front. Clarke went through such lengths to get this accurate that he consulted the British rocket engineer Alan Bond, now famous for the creation of the British Interplanetary Society Project Daedalus and the Reaction Engines Ltd Skylon spaceplane. Clarke also contributed to the early BIS Moonship design in the 1930s. Clarke not only featured spaceships in his science fiction literature, but he also spent considerable time coming up with credible concepts that perhaps someday, may become reality.

In the following two essays, we see how science fiction and spacecraft design are closely linked together and indeed both motivate the other. The first is an essay by Stephen Baxter, exploring starship concepts from the science fiction literature. The second is an essay by Kelvin Long, describing the motivations for founding an actual starship design study called Project Icarus.

Spaceship	Title	Year Published	Description
Ares	The Sands of Mars [1]	1951	Atomic drive
Prometheus	Prelude to Space [2]	1951	Nuclear powered ramjet
Archeron	Earthlight [3]	1955	Nuclear-electric spacedrive
Discovery I	2001: A Space Odyssey [4]	1968	Atomic reactor drive
Monolith	2001: A Space Odyssey [4] 2010: Odyssey Two [5]	1968 1982	Von Neumann self-replicating probes
Rama	Rendezvous with Rama [6]	1973	Reactionless space drive
'Sunjammer'	The Wind from the Sun [7]	1972 (1963)	Solar photon sail
Sirius	Imperial Earth [8]	1975	Asymptotic mini-black hole drive
Magellan	The Songs of Distant Earth [9]	1986	Quantum vacuum ramjet
Starholme	The Fountains of Paradise [10]	1979	Reactionless space drive
Goliath	The Hammer of God [11]	1993	Unknown drive type

References

[1]   A.C.Clarke, The Sands of Mars, Sidgwick & Jackson, 1951.

[2]   A.C.Clarke, Prelude to Space, World Editions Inc, 1951.

[3]   A.C.Clarke, Earthlight, Muller, 1955.

[4]   A.C.Clarke, 2001: A Space Odyssey, New American Library, 1968.

[5]   A.C.Clarke, 2010: Odyssey Two, Granada Publishing, 1982.

[6]   A.C.Clarke, Rendezvous with Rama, Gollancz, 1973.

[7]   A.C.Clarke, 'The Wind from the Sun', Boy's Life Magazine, 1972 (short story orig. pub. 1964).

[8]   A.C.Clarke, Imperial Earth, Gollancz, 1975.

[9]   A.C.Clarke, The Songs of Distant Earth, Del Rey, 1986.

[10] A.C.Clarke, The Fountains of Paradise, Victor Gollancz, 1979.

[11] A.C.Clarke, The Hammer of God, Victor Gollancz, 1993.

Blueprints for a Starship

by Stephen Baxter

"Robot probes – flashing through nearby star systems and radioing back their observations during a few hectic hours of transit … Barring accidents, they would continue speeding through the galaxy forever …" Clarke, *The Songs of Distant Earth*, 1986.

As Project Icarus (see article below) enters its next stage we will, slowly but surely, move towards a precise quantitative design for our hypothetical interstellar probe.

But some interstellar craft in science fiction have featured remarkably detailed and plausible designs – not surprisingly, as many of them derived from work by, or were even written by, experts in the field. What can we learn from these fictional precedents?

In what follows I'm going to focus on ships of the Icarus/Daedalus class, very loosely speaking – that is, no much-slower-than-light multi-generation worldships, as featured from Heinlein's *Universe* [1] to Greg Bear's recent, and excellent, *Hull Zero Three* [2], and no faster-than-light behemoths like *Star Trek*'s *Enterprise*, probably the most detailed fictional starship of all, or the Alcubierre-drive starship of my own *Ark* [3] (2009). As this is a fairly informal essay I haven't overloaded it with specific technical references, but I've included pointers to sources where appropriate, mostly via Matloff's recent survey [4].

Origins

Paul Gilster's excellent *Centauri Dreams* [5] is, among other things, a good source of information on starships in science fiction. The earliest interstellar journey Paul identifies is by a French writer called C.L. Defontenay, dating from 1854; the ship was driven by a kind of antigravity. In science fiction's pulp era of the early twentieth century, various fanciful space drives featured in the fiction of writers like E. E Doc Smith, whose pioneering space opera *Skylark of Space* (1928) [6] appears to have featured a kind of inertial drive.

What was the first *credible* starship design in fiction? The earliest identified by Gilster [5] is a kind of solar sail, in a book called *The Extraordinary Adventures of a Russian Scientist* by the French writers Georges le Faure and Henri de Graffigny, published in 1889-91. It was after the quest for scientific rigour in science fiction pioneered by the great *Astounding Science Fiction* editor John W. Campbell from the late 1930s that starships of a more or less realistic design began to appear regularly in the genre.

Lightsails

Maybe it's no surprise that the first realistic fictional starship was a lightsail. As far as I'm aware this is the only candidate interstellar propulsion technology whose underlying principles were thoroughly defined and indeed demonstrated by the end of the nineteenth century [5]. Paul Gilster highlights an early and memorable depiction of a solar sail ship in Cordwainer Smith's 1960 story *The Lady Who Sailed the Soul* [7]. But it was probably Clarke's 1964 story *The Wind from the Sun* [8] that cemented the idea in the public consciousness.

Rigorous developments of the technology as a means of interstellar travel began with the work of Robert L. Forward. An early use of Forward's ideas was by Niven and Pournelle in their 1974 novel *The Mote in God's Eye* [9]. Aliens from a star known as the Mote launch a 450,000-ton craft across 35 light years (ly) at 7% of c (lightspeed) to the human-occupied *New Caledonia* system. The *Moties* use a laser-pushed lightsail; the sail is thousands of kilometres across and the laser blasts for 45 years. On its approach the ship itself is visible; it decelerates using the light of New Cal's Sun, which is reflected back blue-shifted (details [9] chapters 4 and 6). Forward however felt the authors glossed over the difficulties of deceleration: 'I had warned them that the light from the Sun was not strong enough to stop the sail, but, being science fiction writers ... they ignored my advice and pretended it would work' [5].

Forward first presented his own deceleration design in the pages of a novel, *Rocheworld* [10], before writing it up for technical publication. In the 2020s, the twenty-strong crew of the *Prometheus*, the first manned starship, are to be propelled to Barnard's Star by 'a solar-system-wide machine that would toss them to the stars on a beam of light'. Forward goes into great technical detail, including graphs and diagrams.

Brighton 1987, David Brin, Fred Clarke, Charles Sheffield and Robert Forward

The ship will make a forty-year, one-way journey across six light years to the target star. The payload massing approximately 3500 tons is to be dragged by a sail 1000 km wide; total launch mass is around 82,000 tons. The core of the propulsion system is a set of a thousand laser stations, *each* 30 km wide, in Sun-synchronous orbit around Mercury. These together convert solar energy into laser beams with a combined total power of 1300 TW. The beams are united by a *beam combiner* at Mercury's L-2 point, and ultimately passed through a 300-km transmitter lens between Saturn and Uranus. Forward's ingenious deceleration method is to split the craft's sail in two; a torus, detached from a central section, goes ahead of the craft, collects a fresh 2-year burst of laser light from the solar system, and reflects it back on the residual 300 km-diameter sail still attached to the ship, thus slowing it down.

Forward always thought big – and *Rocheworld* shows Forward's imagination at its staggering best. However the design brings vulnerabilities, as Forward dramatises. The propulsion system needs continuous support on the ground for decades; in the end political opposition nearly kills the project.

Encounter with Tiber, a 1996 novel by Apollo 11 astronaut Buzz Aldrin with science fiction veteran John Barnes [11], is about visits to Earth by *Tiberians*, natives of Alpha Centauri, fleeing disastrous impact events in that system. Two generations of starfaring technology are used by the Tiberians: solar sails, and later *zero-point energy lasers* (of which more later). Gregory Matloff, who contributed to the theoretical development of interstellar solar sailing [4], was a consultant on the book, and the result shows in the detail depicted.

The starship *Wahkopem Zomos* is a stubby cylinder approximately 20 m high with a habitat ring, rotated for artificial gravity. (The distances are my estimates from the text; the ship is described in alien units!) At launch it is connected to a booster stack approximately 100 m tall; an antimatter reaction creates a plasma rocket to drive the ship towards its Sun, Alpha Centauri A, where its solar sail approximately 1000 km wide is unfurled for a perihelion manoeuvre. After a *second* perihelion push at Alpha B, the ship is driven further by lasers. Ultimately the ship reaches around 0.4c. Deceleration is achieved by a 'brakeloop' of superconducting filament approximately 100 km across; this ionises the interstellar medium, thus converting the ship's kinetic energy to heat. The ship was to be brought back from Sol using a laser beam fired from Alpha Centauri and reflected from a separately launched 5000 km mirror sail. In the event political opposition causes this system to be abandoned, stranding the crew until a more advanced ship comes to fetch them.

Rockets

Lightsails are beautiful and the ride comes for free – but rockets are more fun! In my own novel *Space* [12] my hero Reid Malenfant uses a Daedalus-type pulsed-fusion rocket to make a one-way dash to an interstellar teleport node.

The ultimate rocket fuel is of course antimatter. An antimatter rocket launches the AXIS probe (*A*utomated e*X*plorer of *I*nterstellar *S*pace) to Alpha Centauri in Greg Bear's *Queen of Angels* [13]. The journey takes fifteen years; for the first four years the probe is accelerated by the products of an antimatter-matter reaction, and then nanotechnology is used to manufacture huge 'superconducting wings' which decelerate the probe through drag from the Galaxy's magnetic field. In an afterword Bear refers to Forward's work on antimatter drives, and work by Matloff and Fennelly on the deceleration technique [4]. Bear gives only one precise figure about his ingenious ship, and that's the cost: one hundred billion dollars.

Another antimatter rocket features in one of the more detailed starship designs in recent science fiction: the *Venture Star* of James Cameron's 2009 movie *Avatar*. Cameron and his consultants did a good deal of research and design work on the ship, as on many aspects of the movie, not all of which shows up on screen; however background material has been published in various tie-in media [14].

The *Venture Star* is one of a fleet of interstellar ferries, each designed to carry 200 passengers to Pandora, most of them in 'cryosleep' – and including 'avatars', the human-native hybrid bodies used to explore the Moon. On its return it carries 350 tons of cargo, much of it the precious superconducting mineral 'unobtainium', which is essential for antimatter containment.

The ship is over a kilometre long, much of which consists of a strut to separate the habitable compartments from the *hybrid deuterium fusion / matter-antimatter engine*. The ship is launched from the solar system with a laser push on a 'photon sail' 16 km in diameter. During the launch a 'mirror shield' protects the crew compartments from the laser; during the cruise phase at 0.7c this is deployed as a shield against the interstellar medium. Deceleration is achieved using the antimatter engine. This flight sequence is reversed for the return trip.

Bussard Ramjets

The trouble with rockets is that you need to carry fuel. When it was first proposed in 1960 the beauty of the Bussard ramjet [4] was that it appeared to offer ultra-fast interstellar travel without the need to carry any fuel at all. Ramjets featured in the science fiction of Larry Niven almost from Bussard's first publication. The mighty *Ringworld* used ramjets as attitude stabilisers [15]. Excitement reached fever pitch when Carl Sagan, for example, examined an arbitrarily long ramjet journey at an acceleration of 1g; he found that thanks to time dilation the ship could reach the boundary of the visible universe within the lifetime of a crew member [16].

Unfortunately, further studies into the ramjet design indicated that such marvellous dreams are probably impractical. Modified ramjet designs appeared, but these lacked the power, and indeed the romance, of the original notion. In *Footfall*, written by Niven with Pournelle [17], the *fithp*, invaders from Alpha Centauri, travel in what appears to be a modified ramjet of the 'ram augmented interstellar rocket' (RAIR) kind. The *Message Bearer* is a mile-long cylinder, surrounded by a metallic band that appears to be the core of the ramjet system. The ship was launched with a vast spherical fuel tank attached to the nose, evidently fuel for fusion reactors which use the interstellar medium as reaction matter. The ship is turned halfway to Sol to use the ramscoop for deceleration. The mother ship incidentally carries warships which appear to use Daedalus-type pulsed-fusion drives; these are also used to manoeuvre the mother ship.

It takes several *fithp* generations for *Message Bearer* to cross from the nearest star. So much for ramjets! But the disillusion with the idea did not come early enough to quash the inspiration for what many readers regard as the quintessential starflight novel.

Poul Anderson's *Tau Zero* [18] – the novel after which of course the *Tau Zero Foundation* was named – was surely inspired by Sagan's visionary calculations. The starship *Leonora Christine* with its 50 crew sets off on an exploratory mission to Beta Virginis 32 light years away. The ship, like "*a dagger pointed at the stars*", comes with a gym and swimming pool! Under an ion drive it spirals out from Earth orbit at 0.1g. When it has achieved sufficient velocity the Bussard unit opens up at the rear of the craft: "*the scoopfield webs … glistened in the Sunlight, silver across starry black*". These webs are the root of a 'field of magnetohydrodynamic forces' thousands of kilometres across. The fields also serve as shields from the interstellar medium. Crucially, there are separate acceleration vs. deceleration ramjet systems.

A few light years out, calamity strikes. The ship hits a fast-moving nebula – and, already moving at a high percentage of light speed ('low tau'), the crew find their deceleration system is wrecked. To go outside the ship to make repairs they would need to turn the acceleration system off – but that would take down the shields too, killing the crew. The ship must go on ever faster, time dilation becoming ever stronger, until the distances and times travelled become cosmological: *"We will not be able to stop before the death of the universe ... I propose we go on to the next cycle of the cosmos"*. Much of the book is dated now – the Bussard physics, the cosmology. But the sheer sense of wonder never dates; and many researchers into interstellar flight cite *Tau Zero* as a specific inspiration for their careers.

Vacuum Energy

What about more exotic drives? The exploitation of vacuum energy as a star drive seems to have been pioneered by Charles Sheffield in his story *All the Colours of the Vacuum* (1981) [19]. This is fun hard science fiction written by a physicist, but the drive's details are a bit vague: *"The available [vacuum] energies made up a quasi-continuous "spectrum" ... Tuned resonators in the .. drive units selected certain wavelengths which were excited by the corresponding components in the vacuum self-energy. These "colours," as McAndrew thought of them, could feed vacuum energy to the drive system ..."*

The vacuum energy (aka zero point energy) drive in *Encounter with Tiber* by Aldrin and Barnes [11], based on work by Matloff who consulted on the novel [4], works by manipulating the Casimir effect – the one way we do know to extract the energy. Little specific detail is given, but you get a sense of the fragility of a drive generated by manipulating plates held a few atomic diameters apart.

Vacuum energy was most famously exploited by Clarke in his 1986 novel *The Songs of Distant Earth* [20]. Fleeing the impending nova explosion of the Sun, the *Magellan* leaves for a star more than a hundred light years away. Essentially a cylinder four kilometres long, and carrying a small conscious crew supervising a million frozen sleepers, *Magellan* is driven at 0.2c by a *quantum ramjet*. In his acknowledgements Clarke cites papers by Froning in *JBIS* and elsewhere [4] for speculation on the use of vacuum energies for propulsion, but he is even vaguer than Sheffield in the details of how the drive works. In the engine room we glimpse only 'the shrouded metal and crystal shapes, the curiously-formed flying buttresses springing from the walls of the chamber, the pulsing constellations of lights, the sphere of utter blackness that, even though it was completely featureless, somehow seemed to be spinning ... "*One day it will make us masters of the Galaxy*".

However, with assistance from Alan Bond of the BIS, Clarke went into interesting detail on one often-neglected aspect of star missions: the ablation shielding required to protect such a craft from the interstellar medium. To travel approximately 50 light years at 0.2c the *Magellan* requires approximately 100,000 tons of water ice moulded into a conical shield. In this book the shielding actually drives the story; to replenish the ice the *Magellan* is forced to call at an Earthlike planet called Thalassa 50 light years from Earth, previously colonised by a 'seedship'; the plot develops from the interaction of the Thalassans with the starship crew.

An Armada of Dreams

For fun the table summarises the characteristics of some of these paper starships, with Daedalus as a comparison [21].

One impression that stands out from these careful dramatisations is how appallingly difficult interstellar travel is. Schemes based on current or near-future technologies are huge, elaborate, rickety, fragile – the thousands of laser stations, the sails and lenses the size of Moons. We even have to combine technologies; we put lightsails on antimatter rockets. There is surely only so far you can take this. Once the ancient Greeks put sails on rowing boats, but the result was not a nuclear submarine. On the other hand, Columbus's ships were inadequate to meet the challenges of an Atlantic crossing – but he went anyway.

And in the pages of a novel you glimpse the sheer mine-bending scale of the engineering needed. Forward's mighty laser beam was visible from Barnard's Star [10], and Clarke's quantum-ramjet *Magellan* is still visible as a 3rd magnitude star some 15 light years out [20]. How wonderful to imagine human engineering visible across interstellar distances.

Parameter	Daedalus [21]	'Crazy Eddie Probe' [9]	Prometheus [10]	Wahkopem Zomos [11]	Venture Star [14]	Message Bearer [17]	Leonora Christine [18]	Magellan [20]
Source	Human	Motie	Human	Tiberian	Human	Fithp	Human	Human
Date	Late C21	3017	2020s	7000BC	2154	1980s	~2500?	3800
Destination	Barnard's Star	'New Caledonia System' (35ly from Mote)	Barnard's Star	Sol (from Alpha Cen)	Alpha Cen	Sol (from Alpha Cen)	Beta Vir (32ly)	'Sagan 2' (100ly)
Duration	48y		40y		~6y (subj)	Generations	~5y (subj)	500y
Cruise speed	0.12c	0.07c	0.15c	0.4c	0.7c		~c	0.2c
Dimensions	54,000t	450,000t; sail ~1000s km	Payload 3500t, total at launch 82000t	20m-long payload	Length 1.6km, payload 350t	1 mile long		4km long
Crew		1 Motie plus miniatures	20		~200 (most sleepers)		50	1 million (sleepers)
Primary propulsion	Fusion pellets	Lightsail, laser and solar	Lightsail, 1300TW laser	1000km solar sail, EM braking	16km lightsail, antimatter drive	RAIR	Bussard ramjet	Quantum ramjet
Secondary propulsion				Plasma rocket		Pulsed fusion	Ion drive	
Shielding	64m dia., 9mm thick beryllium				Mirror shield		Bussard field	100,000t of water ice

References

[1]   R. Heinlein, *Universe*, Astounding Science Fiction, May 1941.
[2]   G. Bear, *Hull Zero Three*, Orbit, 2010.
[3]   S. Baxter, *Ark*, Gollancz, 2009.
[4]   G.L. Matloff, *Deep Space Probes*, Springer, 2010.
[5]   P. Gilster, *Centauri Dreams*, Springer, 2004.
[6]   E.E. Smith, *Skylark of Space*, Amazing Stories, 1928.
[7]   C. Smith, 'The Lady Who Sailed the Soul', *Galaxy*, 1960.
[8]   A.C. Clarke, 'The Wind from the Sun', *Boy's Life* Magazine, March 1964.
[9]   L. Niven and J. Pournelle, *The Mote in God's Eye*, Simon & Schuster, 1974.
[10]   R. Forward, *Rocheworld*, Baen Books, 1990 (first pub. 1982, much expanded edition 1990).
[11]   B. Aldrin, J. Barnes, *Encounter with Tiber*, Warner, 1996.
[12]   S. Baxter, *Space*, HarperCollins, 2000.
[13]   G. Bear, *Queen of Angels*, Warner Books, 1990.
[14]   M. Wilhelm and D. Mathison, *James Cameron's Avatar: Activist Survival Gde*, HarperCollins, 2009.
[15]   L. Niven, *Ringworld*, Ballantine, 1970.
[16]   I. Shklovskii and C. Sagan, *Intelligent Life in the Universe*, Holden-Day, Inc, 1966.
[17]   L. Niven and J. Pournelle, *Footfall*, Del Rey, 1985.
[18]   P. Anderson, *Tau Zero*, Doubleday, 1970.
[19]   C. Sheffield, 'All the Colours of the Vacuum', *Analog*, 1981.
[20]   A.C. Clarke, *The Songs of Distant Earth*, Del Rey, 1986.
[21]   A. Bond et al, *Project Daedalus Final Report*, British Interplanetary Society, 1978.

Creating a Self-Fulfilling Prophecy in Space

by Kelvin F. Long

The title of this article reflects the motivation behind much of what the writer Arthur C. Clarke achieved throughout his life, and reflected in his vision of a positive future for a united humanity in the peaceful exploration of space. I had the good fortune to meet Arthur C. Clarke at the London Science Museum during a chance encounter. It is a memory that holds particular poignancy for me since we were standing close to the Apollo 10 re-entry module. This struck me as being warmly fitting since I was standing next to one of the great space visionaries who, arguably, helped galvanize public support for space exploration. Despite having only a brief conversation with him, I had already been inspired by his writings, and had long since made the decision to devote my life's work to pursuing our common goal – the exploration of space.

Clarke began writing at a young age and went on to produce many books examining technical problems relating to rockets, lunar exploration and interplanetary travel. Among these books were: *Exploration of The Moon*, *The Making of a Moon*, *Prelude to Space* and *Interplanetary Flight*, a book which Carl Sagan acknowledged had influenced him as a young teenager. Many of Clarke's earlier books contained wonderful drawings from the British space artist Ralph Smith. He followed in the footsteps of the Father of modern space art, the American Chesley Bonestell, who had worked with Wernher von Braun to produce his own magnificent visions of space exploration, so beautifully captured in those famous 1950s *Colliers* magazines articles "*Man Will Conquer Space Soon*".

Clarke played a fundamental role in the early years of the British Interplanetary Society (BIS) both before and after the Second World War and if it wasn't for his efforts (and others) in sustaining its energy once the London branch had been formed it may not have continued. This resulted in many technical studies including the BIS Space Ship and his personal 1945 article "*Extra Terrestrial Relays*" for *Wireless World* magazine which laid the foundations for the communications satellite, thus achieving one of his aims to bring together a global community with a shared ideal of space exploration, rather than focussing on our many divisions.

Influenced by the writings of authors including Olaf Stapledon, who wrote numerous science fiction classics including *Last & First Men* and *Starmaker*, Clarke also turned his attention to science fiction and left a legacy that will inspire millions for generations to come, including books such as *Childhood's End*, *The Fountains of Paradise*, *Rendezvous with Rama*, *The Songs of Distant Earth* and *The City and the Stars*. For many people in the public not widely familiar with science fiction, Clarke will probably be best remembered for his book *2001: A Space Odyssey*, and the film of the same name directed by Stanley Kubrick. What a wonderful collection of literature these works represent – dealing with the obvious challenges facing our species in the exploration of space! How do we travel across the vastness of space? Are we alone in this rather large universe?

In many of his books the human protagonist was often up against something bigger than themselves, something wonderful: an unknown and mysterious cylindrical vessel passing through our solar system; superior artificial intelligence; an intelligent species from another world. But, with the obstacles, was always the hope and optimism that somehow the human could survive the experience, could push through and find the answers to the riddle at hand and perhaps gain a deeper understanding of the nature of the universe itself. In the excellent authorised biography by Neil McAleer titled *Visionary* Clarke makes it clear that he views the purpose of humanity as the processing of information. He also believed that humans were just a stepping-stone on the evolutionary path to artificial intelligence or what he called *Homo electronicas*. Whether one shares this view is a matter of opinion but many educated writers have considered the possibility of a technological singularity and if such an event did occur (some may argue it has already started) then a trend towards artificial intelligence is not an unreasonable extrapolation.

When Clarke died in 2008 he left a worldwide network of admirers. Some just admired his work and see it as good entertainment. But he is also greatly admired by many for his knowledge of science and engineering which he used in many of his stories to create realistic and credible futures for the imagination to digest. This was due to Clarke having an interest in science from a young age and after the war he went on to complete a Physics degree at King's College, London. Many of his technical papers were later published in the book *Ascent to Orbit*. A large number of his science fiction books focused on the technology rather than the characterisation, and much of his works belong in the genre of hard science fiction. An exception to this is *The Songs of Distant Earth*, which although it contains a lot of science, has a very human focus, including a love romance. Some consider this to be Clarke's greatest work; this author's favourite is probably *The City and the Stars*.

Others take his vision more seriously than just entertainment, and re-solve to dedicate their life to making his vision a reality to create a self-fulfill-ing prophecy. Such people are what this author refers to as children of Clarke, creations of his imagination manifested in the minds of real people. Indeed, many science fiction authors such as Stephen Baxter and Gentry Lee were both inspired and mentored by Clarke in their writing, an acknowledgement by Clarke that he needed to actively encourage the continuation of his work in others.

This same philosophy is right for the technical study of interstellar travel – a topic which can take years to master and to become adequately familiar with various propulsion schemes, or indeed how to conduct engineering cal-culations around them. The best way to achieve this is for new recruits in the field to be immersed in design calculations, guided by those with experience.

Thus we come to the origin of Project Icarus, an engineering design study of an interstellar probe. This exciting design study, if successful, aims to pro-duce to a high quality, a set of research reports on the Icarus vehicle con-figuration and mission profile. This could be a highly valuable contribution to the field of interstellar travel. The 1970s Project Daedalus initiative to design an interstellar probe was arguably successful in producing a credible design. Where Project Daedalus showed that interstellar travel was possible in theory (proof of an existence theorem), Project Icarus aims to demonstrate it is theo-retically possible in practice, not by building the vehicle but by demonstrating that the design is sufficiently credible and possible in the near-term.

But Project Icarus is about more than just designing a vehicle. It is also about keeping the vision of humans in space alive for our generation and the next; a necessary requirement if we are to move forward incrementally towards the stars. For such a vision must be continually renewed if it is to be sustained, matured and eventually achieved. Compatible with this vision are two of the non-technical purposes behind Project Icarus: firstly, to generate a greater interest in the real-term prospects for interstellar precursor missions that are based on credible science, and secondly, to motivate a new generation of scientists to be interested in designing space missions that go beyond our solar system. To achieve these requires continuing inspiration and this is how Project Icarus came about.

The interstellar community is a small one and many of its active researchers are nearing, or in, retirement. At the same time the field of interstellar research is a large topic, with many different technical subjects to become familiar with, including multiple propulsion schemes for achieving interstellar travel. Given this situation how can we best encourage replenishment of people in the interstellar community, whilst at the same time making them capable designers, able to undertake engineering calculations to assess different proposals and contribute technically to the field? When pondering this situation it was realised that the best way to achieve this was to organise an international design study of a specific vehicle configuration. Once assembled, this team would slowly become familiar with the literature, make contact with the leaders in the field and eventually become independent and capable researchers on topics relating to interstellar flight. That generation would then go on to continue this vision for another generation and so the momentum towards interstellar travel continues, until a final vehicle engineering blueprint does exist and the long-held goal is achieved.

Project Daedalus was chosen as the logical vehicle for re-design, as it was already an icon of inspiration within the field and so why not utilise the same vehicle for this purpose, which was in drastic need of revision anyway given the scientific advances in the fields of materials technology, nanotechnology, electronics, fusion research and astronomical observations? This was how the vision of Arthur C. Clarke was to be exercised in a practical way, with a real output to be delivered not just in the form of technical reports but also in the creation of starship designers for the decades ahead. This led to the founding of Project Icarus, launched at a British Interplanetary Society symposium in September 2009.

The Project Icarus Study Group is a truly international endeavour, with designers coming from all across the globe. This is consistent with the way that space missions today and in the future are to be conducted. This is also an acknowledgement that when the first interstellar probe is eventually launched it will be representing all humans on Earth and not just a single nation-state. Alien life in the Universe may come in many varied forms, intelligent species which view our planet, will not look at us through discrete nation-state eyes, but instead judge us as a single continuous species of humans with many flaws, but with a great hope for our future that we can solve our problems on Earth and continue this trend into space and onwards to the nearby stars. Perhaps with our talent for problem-solving, we may be able to address wider problems that may exist for all species in the galaxy and beyond; our potential contribution to the collection of galactic intelligence is limitless, should such a community of worlds indeed exist. This is the self-fulfilling prophecy that Arthur C. Clarke hoped to motivate. If the Project Icarus Study Group can contribute towards this positive future for our species then we will have achieved our objective.

If old *"Spaceship"* (or *"Ego"* as Clarke was also known) was still alive today, then it is hoped that he would be proud of our efforts in wanting to make the world a better place now and wanting to provide for a positive human future in space in the centuries ahead. In the meantime, some of us will have to ensure we live until the year 2058 (which may require Artificial Intelligence enhancements) when the *Clarkives* are finally opened, a set of documents containing Clarke's personal notebooks, letters and perhaps further personal reflections on the future of our species. If it contained any short story sequels such as to his Odyssey series then this would be one of the longest-recorded sequels in the history of literature. It would be a fitting tribute to Clarke if our species had by then fully explored our solar system and was taking its first steps towards the stars. Our childhood would indeed have come to an end and our minds set on the path to adulthood where perhaps others await our anticipated arrival. Ultimately, this is what Project Icarus is all about.

(Originally written for Project Icarus, 2011)

Chapter IX - The Father to the Man

by Stephen Baxter

I grew up with the works of Sir Arthur C Clarke, which had a profound effect on my own work and my thinking. And I was privileged to get to know Clarke personally, especially from 1996 when we began to collaborate on fiction projects. We eventually produced four novels: the standalone *The Light of Other Days* (2000), and the three-novel *Time Odyssey* sequence: *Time's Eye*, *Sunstorm* and *Firstborn* (2004-8).

In the course of our work together we always spoke much more of the future than of the past. It was in Clarke's nature to look forward rather than back. And yet it always seemed clear to me that, as it is for all of us, much of Clarke's fiction was profoundly influenced by his boyhood and youth.

I first met Clarke in 1992, when my first novel *Raft* was nominated for the Arthur C. Clarke Award for best science fiction novel of the year. I didn't win but was the only nominee to turn up at the ceremony, which was held in Minehead, Clarke's birthplace in Somerset, to celebrate his 75th birthday. I and my wife met Clarke through the kindness of Clarke's brother Fred, who has always been a great supporter of his brother, and indeed a friend to us.

My publishers sent Clarke copies of my next few novels, and Clarke was particularly taken by *The Time Ships* (1995), my sequel to Wells's *The Time Machine*. He responded with a kind blurb, and with correspondence: he sent me a copy of the HG Wells Society magazine, and even a little collectors' postcard of Wells himself. This was enormously generous; Clarke was almost exactly forty years older than me, and had no need even to notice writers of my generation. And there was a sense of British science fiction continuity for me. Clarke never met Wells himself, but he did know Olaf Stapledon, who was a friend of Wells. And now here I was corresponding with Clarke.

A couple of years later I interviewed Clarke for *SFX* Magazine, by phone and e-mail. Out of that, at my suggestion, grew our first collaboration, a short story which eventually sold to *Playboy*. That was how my name entered the frame a couple of years later when Clarke was looking for a new collaborator for the book which became *The Light of Other Days*. Of course I was not Clarke's first collaborator; for example he had worked on sequels to *Rendezvous with Rama* with Gentry Lee. In later years Clarke, afflicted by post-polio syndrome, did not always have the strength to fulfil his ideas alone.

On all of our books, starting from fairly open-ended outlines by Clarke, we kicked around ideas and outlines for some months before getting down to work, corresponding by e-mail and phone. I didn't actually meet Clarke again in person after that Minehead event. Our last project together was a new short story in the *Tales of the White Hart* universe for a new edition of those tales from PS Publishing. These projects were a great pleasure for me. It was a privilege to work with a man who had such a profound influence on my life, and the work was a stimulating joy in its own right.

Clarke was already in his eighties when we began these projects. Even in old age, Clarke was always fascinated by the new, by the endlessly unfolding novelty of the universe revealed by science – as well as in the newest science fiction; I remember him mentioning his reading of Geoff Ryman and China Mieville in this period. As I said, his focus was always much more on the future than on the past. And yet it always seemed to me that the influence of his boyhood and youth was never far away.

Consider our second Time Odyssey novel, *Sunstorm*, in which a disorderly Sun threatens Earth. This grew out of an outline by Clarke provisionally called *Nova*, which he had tinkered with for many years. The misbehaviour of the Sun had featured in many of Clarke's works, beginning with *Rescue Party* (1946), and including his novel *The Songs of Distant Earth* (1986) in which mankind has a thousand-year warning of the Sun going 'nova' and scatters to the stars.

These works, and similar solar-threat stories by other writers, reflect a primal human perception. Perhaps we moderns are too blasé about the Sun. We understand a lot more about the Sun than our ancestors ever did, but we are just as dependent on its power: if the Sun flickers, so does our climate. For over seventy years, from around 1640 to 1710, very few sunspots were observed on the Sun's face, and the Earth was plunged into what the climatologists call the "Little Ice Age", when London children ice-skated on the Thames. Today our dependence on high technology makes us vulnerable to even mild solar tantrums. A flare once knocked out communications on Air Force One; on 24th April 1984 President Reagan, over the mid-Pacific, was left incommunicado for two hours.

And Arthur Clarke, co-author of *Sunstorm*, grew up on farms, utterly reliant on the weather, and the light of the Sun. Indeed, from the age of thirteen after the death of his father, Clarke as the eldest son had to shoulder a large burden in the running of a farm. When he was a boy, the farm was without electricity; he would walk or cycle to and from school in the dark. In a way unimaginable to those of us of later urban generations, Clarke, who we think of as a thoroughly modern figure, grew up rooted in nature, embedded in the cycles of light and day. I have always wondered if his fascination with misbehaving-Sun stories was a faint echo of the perceptions of that farm boy, wedded to the Earth and dependent on the Sun as farmers had been for ten thousand years.

But the world into which farmer's-boy Clarke was born was changing fast. Born in 1917, Clarke lived through the great expansion of urbanisation and industrialisation which transformed much of Britain (and the US) in the decades 1890s-1930s – in many parts of Britain terminating an agricultural tradition that had roots all the way back to the Iron Age. His father, a telephone engineer (telecommunications engineering was deep-rooted in Clarke's family background) brought the telephone to his own farm.

And when boyhood ended and war came, Clarke was exposed with shocking suddenness to very high technology and its implications. During the Second World War Clarke (aged twenty-two in 1939) rose to the rank of flight-lieutenant in the RAF. Much of his work concerned pioneering developments in radar.

This Sundering from his agricultural past was documented interestingly in Clarke's fiction, in the semi-autobiographical novel *Glide Path* (1963). Through the hyper-advanced technology of the war whiz-kid radar engineer Alan Bishop has encountered a new level of reality: "He had become entangled in powers and instrumentalities that would surely shape the future" (chapter 30). When he is called back to his father's funeral in Clarke's West Country, Bishop finds he has outgrown his home: "He could never escape from [his childhood's] influence, for it had shaped his character irrevocably ... But it would no longer dominate him". Perhaps this wartime-crisis experience of sudden personal growth and exposure to high technology also, more subtly, influenced Clarke's many tales of transcendence through technology, from *Childhood's End* (1953) to *2001* (1968) and beyond: *"just as Bishop leaves his rural childhood for a technocratic future, so mankind must one day leave the green cradle of Earth."*

Of course Clarke's discovery of science fiction was perhaps the single most significant event of his boyhood. In a sense this occurred not once but twice, when he discovered the vigorous American pulp tradition through chance encounters with American science fiction magazines from age 11, and then when he found the works of the British writer Olaf Stapledon at age 12. And you can trace these influences in his works.

Clarke and I thought of our *Time Odyssey* project as a sort of right-angled follow-up to the *Space Odyssey* series: an 'orthoquel', dealing with some of the same themes in a quite different manner. So, while we worked on *Time Odyssey*, I went back several times to re-read the four books of the original Odyssey series, *2001: A Space Odyssey* (1968), *2010: Odyssey Two* (1982), *2061: Odyssey Three* (1987) and *3001: The Final Odyssey* (1997). And I was very struck by the development of these books' visions of space.

Although the movie *2001* was first screened in the year Apollo 8 circled the Moon, its vision was a sort of summary of older dreams of spaceflight. The space clippers and great rotating space wheels were straight out of a blueprint Wernher von Braun had been developing for NASA since the 1950s, while the beautiful, elegant, roomy nuclear ship Discovery was an almost pulp-era vision of how the solar system should have been won.

But by the time *2010* was published in 1982, Apollo was already a ten-years-gone memory, and the space shuttle had just begun flying; we had learned what space is really like. In the novel a new spacecraft called *Leonov* goes to Jupiter to retrieve the lost *Discovery*, and to further mankind's relationship with the monolith-builders. The contrast between the spacecraft old and new is very striking. *Leonov* is an expression of the reality of spaceflight as it had been experienced: it is cramped, uncomfortable, squat, ugly – and there's no gravity-inducing carousel. When the two spacecraft are docked, it's a collision of post-Apollo reality with pre-Apollo dreams, as if two universes are overlapping.

But by *3001*, thanks to the energy-rich 'Inertial Drive' more extravagant spacecraft designs are possible, and old pulp-magazine fantasies are back, which Clarke evokes explicitly. Back-from-the-dead *2001* astronaut Frank Poole says: *"Do you know what Goliath reminds me of? ... When I was a boy, I came across a whole pile of old science-fiction magazines that my Uncle George had abandoned – "pulps", they were called ... They had wonderful garish covers, showing strange planets and monsters – and of course, spaceships! As I grew older, I realised how ridiculous those spaceships were ... Well, those old artists had the last laugh ... Goliath looks more like their dreams than the flying fuel-tanks we used to launch from the Cape."*

Another explicit nod to his boyhood reading habits came with Clarke's 1973 novel *Rendezvous with Rama*. In the year 2131, something sails out of the dark towards the Sun. Astronomers label it Rama, after a Hindu god. *Rama* is unwrapped before our eyes, growing from a star-like telescopic object to an obviously artificial cylinder fifty kilometres long. And when Captain Norton of the Space Survey lands his ship *Endeavour* on *Rama's* axis, we find that this huge spacecraft contains a world, ripe for exploration.

After *2001* Clarke had become probably the best-known science fiction writer on Earth. But having delivered a movie and novel which to many defined the future, in his next novel he turned to a much older form of storytelling. In 1976 he said, "*In Rendezvous with Rama ... I was trying to prove that the traditional adventure story can still carry everything I want to say. In that sense Conan Doyle's The Lost World [1912] is a model of what I mean.*" *Endeavour* was named after Captain Cook's flagship, and *Rama* has human-friendly features like breathable air and 'staircases as high as the Himalayas'. *Rama* is one of Cook's discovered islands, like Hawaii. Or it is Conan Doyle's *Lost World*, transplanted to the sky?

Certainly as an adventure story *Rama* is huge fun. But there are grand ideas on display here too. *Rama* has no crew, but the ship itself, an ultra-intelligent machine, wakes in the sunlight. And when *Rama* finally passes on out of the solar system, having ignored humanity entirely, there is a desolating sense of loss and insignificance. With *Rama* Clarke succeeds in delivering true cosmic wonder by the deceptively simple means of a nostalgic nod to the adventure stories of his youth.

But it was Clarke's primal immersion in the ideas of Stapledon, from a very young boyhood, that resulted in his most sublime works.

Consider his novel *The City and the Stars* (1956). In the opening scene Earth's last city, Diaspar, gleams like a jewel on the desert, closed on itself and tremendously old: "[Its inhabitants] *had walked the same miraculously unchanging streets while more than a thousand million years had worn away*". Clarke is remembered for his ideas, and this book drips with them. But *City* also brings us a rich series of images: the window through Diaspar's walls looking out at the stars, the empty subway station with the single glowing map line leading to one destination, 'LYS' – and Lys itself, a second community, as verdant as Diaspar is mechanical, and hosting children where Diaspar has nothing but frozen electronic ghosts: "*Diaspar had paid, and paid in full, the price of immortality*".

This book of eternity itself had a long conception. Clarke said he began work on early versions while still at school, where he was encouraged greatly by a sympathetic teacher, a World War One veteran called Mr Mitford to whom Clarke later dedicated a volume of short stories. The elements of the story grew slowly over the years, out of that boyhood root. *"Because it was my firstborn,"* Clarke wrote in a 1990 introduction, "[the book] *has always had a special place in my affections, yet I was never completely satisfied with it."* The title of the first published version, *Against the Fall of Night*, was taken from an AE Housman poem. Suitably enough for a book dominated by striking images, the opening scene of that early version, of a last cloud evaporating over a desert city, came to Clarke *"out of nowhere"* in 1936 at age 19. He wrote several drafts before his war service, but a 1946 draft was rejected by John Campbell at *Astounding Stories*. This version was finally accepted for serialisation from 1948. Then, during a long sea voyage in 1955, nearly twenty years after that first flash of inspiration, Clarke produced the final form, as *The City and the Stars*.

Clarke was wise to keep working at this material. The final *City* is much the better version. And with his repeated reworking Clarke also showed a sound creative instinct, for the book is a clear reaction to his strongest boyhood influence, Stapledon. Indeed *City* reads almost like a sequel to the titanic events of Stapledon's *Last and First Men* (1930) and *Star Maker* (1937), in which a much-evolved mankind joins in a galactic quest to create a cosmic consciousness. In *City* this sort of project resulted in a *Mad Mind* who shattered the Galactic Empire, and Diaspar's long history is actually no more than a *"belated and trivial epilogue"*. But *City* is also a better novel, as a novel, than anything Stapledon ever wrote. *City* remained creatively alive throughout Clarke's life. Gregory Benford produced a fine sequel in 1990, and in 2001 David Bedford's musical interpretation was premiered by the Crouch End Festival Chorus.

A writer's early works, before experience and craft take over, can be a richer expression of his/her deepest influences and subconscious yearnings than later material. By returning in his thirties and in later life to visions from his boyhood, Clarke was revisiting the wellspring of his own creativity.

Stephen Baxter is the author of over four dozen books, some of which he co-authored with Sir Arthur C. Clarke. He is a fellow of the British Interplanetary Society and Vice-President of the H.G. Wells society. He has won over a dozen awards for his writing.

Chapter X - Interplanetary Men

Arthur Clarke and Olaf Stapledon
Cosmic visionaries

by Mark Stewart

"Do you know how they got Stapledon to do that lecture?" asked Bob Parkinson. We were standing in the kitchen at the BIS, just before an evening lecture. I shook my head, a little over awed at having a cup of coffee made for me by the President of the BIS. *"Clarke and a few others just went to where he was living at the time,"* explained Bob, *"and knocked on his front door; they just asked him to do it! That's how it happened. That's how we got him to speak."*

London 2011: Many luminaries have given talks at the BIS over the years but few have had more impact on its members than the one delivered by Olaf Stapledon in 1948. Any internet browser will give you a pencil sketch of the man: born May 10 1886 (just nine years before publication of *The Time Machine*) in Seacombe near Liverpool, a noted British philosopher and writer (of both fiction and non-fiction), married with three children, who died unexpectedly of a heart attack in September 1950. But look beyond these hastily drawn details and you find a man who should be far more famous than he is.

Without Stapledon it's unlikely that any of Clarke's Space Odysseys would have been written. Or *Imperial Earth*, *Rendezvous with Rama*, or *The Fountains of Paradise*. And given that Olaf had an equally profound effect on Patrick Moore perhaps there would be no *Sky at Night*, or any of Patrick's books, well over one hundred in total. By any reckoning such omissions would make the world a drearier place.

The world has not forgotten Stapledon; his books are still for sale, both on the high street and on the internet and his importance is still recognised by historians of both science fact and science fiction. One book recently reviewed for *Spaceflight – Cosmos & Culture: Cultural Evolution in a Cosmic Context* – contains a paper on The post-biological Universe. This is a universe that would have been very familiar to Stapledon, for it is one "in which most intelligence has evolved beyond flesh and blood to AI." The paper encourages the reader to engage in "Stapledonian Thinking" in considering issues affecting the evolution of Mankind across cosmic spans of time. This chapter also discusses the possible rise of machine intelligence to the point where it surpasses the human intellect, a familiar theme in the seminal novels of both Stapledon and Clarke.

One of the great unrealised projects of modern cinema is a movie version of one or more of Stapledon's novels. And it will take a cinematic genius – the successor to Stanley Kubrick, or Ridley Scott – to film these stories. But it can and should be done, for few novels lend themselves so readily to the "mythic grandeur" contained in Olaf's cosmic visions. It is time once again to go in search of the *"proverbial good science fiction movie"*, which – with one or two intelligent exceptions *(Blade Runner, Silent Running)* – has rarely been seen in our cinemas since *2001: A Space Odyssey*.

London 1948: a very different world to the one we live in today, one in which cigarettes are considered a harmless sophistication, and trams are still visible in the streets. The skies are different too; strangely quiet and devoid of vapour trails. Very little TV and no commercial radio. And, of course, no internet; not for another forty years or more.

In one of these streets a man makes his way to an evening appointment. He is unremarkable in appearance. He lacks any of the iconic features that will so characterise Albert Einstein in the public imagination, a collective consciousness which will never truly embrace this visionary writer. Perhaps he is a little bookish, there is something of the professor about his clothes and diffident manner, and he would not have drawn a second glance from passers-by. Some legendary figures just don't look like legends. He enters a non-descript building and proceeds to a room reserved for a meeting of the British Interplanetary Society, an organisation still largely unheard of in the post-war years and which lacks a permanent home.

In the audience are a very young Arthur Clarke and an even younger Patrick Moore. And, as its 1948, it's quite possible that other founding members of the Society are also present: possibly the *"brilliant eccentric"* Archie Lowe – the pre-War leader of the BIS; perhaps also the multi-talented Willie Ley (who would go on to co-author books with Chesley Bonestell and Wernher von Braun); the modest and self-effacing Les Shepherd (who helped found the International Astronautical Federation); and the hugely gifted R.A. Smith, whose classic space paintings still adorn the walls at the BIS HQ.

Clarke has already written his ground-breaking and world-changing paper on geosynchronous satellites; but it is still some fifteen years or more before he will team up with Stanley Kubrick to provide cinema goers with a wholly realistic glimpse into the near future. And it is still nine years before Patrick Moore will present the first episode of *The Sky at Night,* a programme which will go on to become the longest running series on British TV. More than any other writer, Stapledon's novels – particularly *Star Maker* and *Last and First Men* – will influence both of these early members of the BIS.

It was Clarke who introduced Olaf's lecture. With little additional preamble Olaf rises to his feet - the typed draft of his presentation shaking slightly in his hands - and begins his talk.

Olaf claimed to be a "dabbler in many subjects, an expert in none." And yet there can be no doubt that he was an expert visionary, and that many of his themes and preoccupations would be taken up by other writers and developed in works of both fact and fiction. The transcript of the talk is full of polite circumlocutions, the sometimes torturous language of a quiet and deferential man caught up in the social conventions of an era very different to ours. But even across a gulf of more than half a century the main themes of that lecture are as topical now as they were then:

On the "age of experts": *"Knowledge has become so vast that no single mind can speak with authority save in relation to his own particular corner of it."*

On nuclear war: "(Mankind's) *folly may quite well lead to the destruction of civilisation, to the extermination of his species, and even to the extinction of all terrestrial life. It is not entirely fantastic to surmise that he may even blow up his planet, and reduce it to a new swarm of asteroids."*

Like Dickens, Olaf believed in the "great common enterprise of man." That *"given a modicum of wisdom, we shall be able greatly to raise the conditions of life for all human beings, no matter what their colour, and to afford to every one of them the chance to develop and express such capacity as he has for truly human living and truly human work in the great common enterprise of man."*

On the future of humanity: *"The river of human life has reached a precipice. The cataract plunges – whither?....There seem to be three possible futures for man: (1) actual and speedy annihilation; (2) the creation of a world-wide totalitarian state, based on atomic power and the reduction of all human individuals to robots; (3) the founding of a new kind of human world , in which the Aladdin's lamp of science will be used wisely...."*

On exotic forms of extra-terrestrial life: *"...might there not be living creatures based not on chemical action but on the energy released by the disintegration of atoms? Might there not be, not on any planet but in the Sun's turbulent outer layers or in its middle depths, flame-like organisms of this type, and might not some species of them equal or excel man in intelligence?"*

On the need for a global space effort: *"Must the first flag to be planted beyond the Earth's confines be the Stars and Stripes, and not the banner of a united Humanity?"*

On the impulse for planetary exploration: *"They (unexplored planets) would offer the kind of lure that was offered in the nineteenth century by Darkest Africa, the north and south poles and the unclimbed Himalayas. Bold young people would be very ready to give their services for planetary exploration. Their effective motive would probably be sheer adventure, though the rational justification of such costly and dangerous undertakings would of course be the advance of science... (and) the hope of discovering* immense fields of natural resources, and exploiting them for human welfare."

On genetic engineering: "If the planets are unadaptable to Man in his present form, perhaps Man might adapt himself to the alien environments of those strange worlds. In fact, given sufficient biological knowledge... it might be possible to breed new human types of men to people the planets. Once more, Mars seems to offer the best opportunity. It should be fairly easy to produce a variety of Homo sapiens capable of surviving the rigours of an improved Martian environment."

On the dangers of genetic engineering: "But a word of caution is necessary. It is extremely important that none of these eugenical ventures should be attempted without thorough knowledge of the probable indirect results of each proposed change.... The result of thoughtless "messing about" with human nature might be the psychological and spiritual ruin of Man."

On the dangers of Utopia: "...there is a point beyond which the increase of luxury leads to spiritual degradation. Man has risen by versatility and intelligence. If he were to enter at last upon a stable condition of perfect adaptation to an unchanging environment, he would gradually lose his distinctive power. Intelligence would atrophy....sooner or later Man would be confronted with some new challenge from the environment, and would have lost the wit to cope with it!"

On the difficulties of interstellar travel and crossing what Wells described as "the gulf of space": "...intelligent races within the cosmos may be forever isolated from each other by the spatial immensities."

With human space exploration facing a prolonged period of uncertainty, the space industry needs visionaries and intelligent futurists now more than ever. There is still much to learn from Olaf's cosmic perspectives, from his unique ability to see far into Deep Time, across vistas that can be measured in millions of years. His works of imaginative fiction allow him to claim a fellowship with Wells, Verne, Clarke and Stanislaw Lem.

Stapledon and Clarke were perhaps the *First Interplanetary Men*. As long as the BIS continues to encourage and inspire they will not be *The Last*.

Chapter XI - Before The Odyssey

by Kelvin F. Long

It was once said by someone that there are some people who live in this world physically, but they exist mentally in the future. Everything they do involves the future, looking forward to the next technological breakthrough or science discovery, and the impact it would have on the human species. Sir Arthur C. Clarke was one of these people. But before he became *The* Arthur C. Clarke, he was just a boy and like many young people his interest in space exploration had to start somewhere. For Arthur, it was the literature works of H.G. Wells and Jules Verne which sparked his imagination. This included books by Verne such as *A Journey to the Centre of the Earth, From the Earth to the Moon* and *Twenty Thousand Leagues Under the Sea*. Books by Wells included *The Time Machine* and *The First Men in the Moon. The War of the Worlds* was the first Wells book that Clarke ever read.

He went on to discover the works of William Olaf Stapledon when he had written several books as a way of communicating his philosophy. *Last and First Men* and *Star Maker* are considered to be the twin pillars of Stapledon's literary career. Clarke first came across *Last and First Men* in 1930 and described it as *"No book before or since ever had such an impact on my imagination"*. Clarke would later meet Stapledon when he invited him to give the British Interplanetary Society lecture in London in 1948, titled *Interplanetary Man* (described in the previous chapter by Mark Stewart.)

There were three other works of literature which were important to Clarke's development and the beginning of his personal Odyssey to a spectacular career as a writer, thinker and all round futurist. These are the pulp magazines *Amazing Stories* and *Astounding Stories* and a little book called *The Conquest of Space*.

Clarke had read the November 1928 issue of *Amazing Stories* at his much older friend's house, a gentleman named Larry Killie, when he was only eleven years old. He was visiting his grandmother's house in Minehead during the school holidays. The cover was painted by the artist Frank R. Paul and depicts a giant Jupiter planet dominating the sky of one of its Moons. A cylindrical shaped spaceship is in the foreground with visitors from Earth pouring out to view the *amazing* site. Despite noticing the magazine cover, Arthur recalls in his science fiction autobiography *Astounding Days* that he doesn't remember it making much impression on him at the time, being only aged eleven.

For a bigger impression he had to wait until he was thirteen when in 1930 he came across the March 1930 issue of *Astounding Stories* magazine. He discovered this in a study room at Huish Grammar School nicknamed, The Dungeon. The cover of *Astounding* was created by Hans Waldermar Wessolowski (Wesso) and depicts a submarine looking spacecraft with a glass-domed observatory, moving towards a strange Moon (it was apparently supposed to be the Moon). The Sun is eclipsed in the bottom left corner by the Earth, with coronal streamers apparent. Clarke said of this cover *"It's a gorgeous cover, and still sets the back of my neck tingling even today"*.

Both the *Amazing Stories* and *Astounding Stories* covers are reproduced below so we can see what early imagery sparked Clarke's imagination. It is worth noting as a footnote that in 1931 when Clarke was aged fourteen, and after discovering *Astounding Stories*, his father passed away. One can only speculate as to what support these magazines of imagination provided him during this difficult time. We can also only guess at what effect the stories contained within these magazines.

Finally, we come to one of the first popular books on space exploration that had a big influence on Clarke, *The Conquest of Space*. David Lasser was born in 1902, a year before the Wright Brothers made their famous first powered flight. In the 1920s he worked as the Editor of Hugo Gernsback's new science fiction magazine, *Science Wonder Stories*. In 1930 he was the founder of the American Interplanetary Society which in 1934 was renamed the American Rocket Society. Later it became *The American Institute of Aeronautics & Astronautics*. *The Conquest of Space* was one of the first serious discussions on astronautics, if not the first. Lasser had a good knowledge of science and engineering from his Bachelor degree at the Massachusetts Institute of Technology (MIT) and was able to use this in writing the book which became an inspiration for generations of science fiction writers including Arthur C. Clarke. In a 2002 introduction to the book Arthur recounts how when he was 14 years old in 1931 he came across the W. H. Smith bookstore in Minehead whilst walking with his Aunt Nelli. This would have been during the summer of 1931. He had an interest in science fiction at that time, but the idea that space travel could be real, as depicted on the cover of the book, intrigued him so much that he persuaded his Aunt to purchase it for him. Arthur recounts how the book *"literally changed my life"*. Clarke praises the book so highly that he refers to David Lasser as *"the first stage booster than launched me into orbit"*.

The book has four sections, dealing with; *The Rocket*, *The Flight Into Space*, *New Worlds*, *By Rockets to the Planets*, Selected Articles and Correspondence. Lasser powerfully explains his motivations for writing the book: *"Among unprejudiced and far-sighted men of science there is agreement today that man has in the rocket an engine to carry him away from Earth, across hundreds of thousands and millions of miles to the Moon, or Mars, or Venus....It is hoped by this presentation of the future of rocket flights in the Earth's atmosphere and in interplanetary space that the mists of misunderstanding, ignorance, and prejudice that surround the 'interplanetary rocket' quest may be cleared up"*.

The book depicts drawings of rocket designs that came out of Germany, including a three-step rocket as proposed by Hermann Oberth. Lasser foresaw many of the commercial, scientific and military applications of the rocket and this insight has been shown to be correct. The commercial launch of satellites, and now space tourists, is an established and emerging industry respectively. Many of these satellites are actually scientific probes, sent into space to observe the Earth or to visit the many planets that inhabit our solar system. The military applications are all too clear, from the development of the German V2 in the 1940s to the Intercontinental Ballistic Missile.

It is difficult to judge how big an influence the David Lasser book was on Clarke, but we can only take him at his word when he says that it changed his life. It is interesting how books like this have inspired great thinkers. In 1950 Clarke published *Interplanetary Flight: An Introduction to Astronautics*, a science book exploring the possibilities of space travel which included an appendix with the equations necessary to understand basic astronautics. This book in particular, influenced another great writer and scientist, the American astronomer Carl Sagan. When Sagan read the book as a teenager, he realized that calculus could be used for something important. Perhaps this is how we best prepare the next generation, by a combination of inspiration and education and a long line of scientists and writers have been influenced in this way. But, David Lasser was one of the first.

Cover of Amazing Stories (November 1928) courtesy of the Frank R. Paul Estate.

Cover of Astounding Stories (March 1930) courtesy of Penny Publications LLC.

Republished Cover of The Conquest of Space by David Lasser (originally published 1931).

First Edition of Olaf Stapledon's Last and First Men from 1930

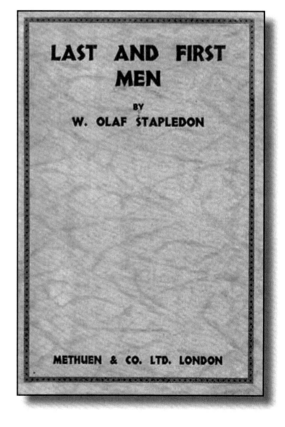

Chapter XII - Beyond 2001 - the Gala

by Robert Godwin

Just as the year 1984 will be forever associated with George Orwell, the year 2001 belongs to Arthur C. Clarke. Both men wrote of a future society, but two more dramatically disparate visions could hardly be imagined. As I write this in 2013 I am keenly aware that although neither of these two visions came to pass, we still seem to be gradually creeping our way towards both contradicting possibilities. One I would welcome gladly and the other I would be equally happy to avoid. While we seem to be able to conjure up vast sums of money to track our every move using machines that make HAL 9000 seem warm and fuzzy, we always seem to be out-of-pocket when it comes to building the sort of spaceship described by Clarke in his legendary novel and movie.

Over forty years ago large nuclear rocket engines were test-fired successfully multiple times in the desert of the American west. Engines that, once launched into space by conventional means, could take us to the moons of Saturn in a manageable timeframe. Arthur C. Clarke knew this very well, way back in the 1930s, and he also knew that without nuclear propulsion we would likely never attain the goal of becoming a multi-planet species. More significantly we now know if we don't do this we might as well sit tight and wait for the asteroid with our name on it.

So 2001 has come and gone, but it will forever be Arthur's year. During that summer twelve years ago I was invited by Rick Tumlinson of the Space Frontier Foundation to become involved in a special event to honour Sir Arthur. It was to take place at the Playboy Mansion in Los Angeles, which to some seemed an incongruous and possibly inappropriate place for such an event. But one must remember that Arthur wrote reams of material for Playboy in the 1960s. There was a long history between Hef and Clarke and despite its tawdry reputation the Mansion had hosted hundreds of fund-raisers over the years attended by people from all walks of life.

I jumped at the chance to be involved and offered my services to edit and publish the event program and to compile a movie to be shown to the guests during dinner. The next few months were a blur of phone calls, emails and Fedex packages and I soon found myself dealing with a madcap array of people who had been inspired by Arthur and wanted to say so in the program.

The date had been set for November 15th 2001 and things were becoming wildly hectic. Then, catastrophe struck in New York City and Washington DC. The worst possible aspects of human nature hammered into the world's consciousness on September 11th. My memories of that day are best kept for another time, but as the true magnitude of what had happened slowly became apparent phones began to ring and people started talking about cancelling our event. Anyone at that time could understand why this was considered. No one knew just how far off the precipice we were about to fall. But as we moved into the month of October sober second thought began to come into play. People were angry but they were also determined to not back down. Nor were we about to let Arthur down. Life had to continue, so planning for the event went ahead as scheduled. With all these years of hindsight I'm glad that we made that decision. Far from being disrespectful of the fallen it felt more like we were rallying around the future that we COULD have, if we were all a bit less parochial in our thinking.

When the night of the event finally arrived although I knew that Arthur wouldn't be in attendance I felt like this was the closest I would ever get to chatting with the magnificent "Ego" of lore. A stunning roster of guests and speakers were lined up for the evening. People from the space community, the science fiction community and the inevitable Hollywood crowd; whose home ground we were now invading. As one of the organisers I knew I was in for a busy evening but even I didn't expect to be whisked away from my wife the second I walked into the Playboy grounds. Tom Huckabee, the director of the evening's events grabbed me before I had even a moment to admire the 12 foot-tall monolith on the front lawn or pose for a photograph with the ape-men grunting around its base. Tom quickly pulled me aside and said, *"Rob you're the only one here who knows all the people from both the space and SF community. Go and round them up and bring them all backstage."* Well, I can tell you, this was not a job for the meek. About five hundred people in black ties and evening gowns were swirling around the gardens and fountains, all in search of a personal moment with those very same celebrities I had been sent to retrieve. Not one of them showed an ounce of sympathy for my plight when I pushed into each huddle and dragged away the centre of their attentions. To this day I am still astounded that the celebrities all complied without so much as a, "So who are you anyway?"

Alan Hale, Bill Paxton and Rob Godwin

Fred Clarke, Bill Paxton and Buzz Aldrin share a moment of levity

Twenty minutes later I found myself huddled under a 60 watt light bulb hanging from a tree, tucked away behind the large Marquee, where dinner was about to be served. Tom then started his roll-call. *"OK. Where's Xander? Right you're the voice of HAL 9000 tonight. You're going up first and you'll be announcing our MC."* Xander Berkeley, one of the stars of the movie Apollo 13 popped up and nodded his head. *"Right Patrick, as soon as Xander announces you, head out to the podium."* Immediately at my elbow the dulcet tones of Patrick Stewart chimed up, *"Right."* I looked at him and he just beamed at me and said, *"Hi!"* I stammered something incomprehensible in reply and glanced across at Pascal Lee, the noted Mars expert who looked back at me with the same expression that I was almost certainly wearing, which said "How did I get *here*?"

This continued for the next five minutes as each person took their instructions from Tom. James Cameron, Morgan Freeman, Buzz Aldrin, Jim Lovell, Fred Clarke, Dan Richter, Alan Hale (fresh off discovering his comet) Frank Drake of SETI and Bill Paxton, who as of that moment was the most bankable movie star in the world now that Titanic was under his belt. Tucked in behind them all was Jeff "Skunk" Baxter of the Doobie Brothers and Steely Dan fame, who was about to provide the live music for the evening.

That moment behind the tent is burned into my memory and yet it doesn't surprise me that such a group of talented people would rally around Arthur's totem for one special evening. Anyway as we were all about to disperse to our designated positions I suggested to Frank Braun, the show's producer, that perhaps we might want to capture the moment for posterity with a photograph. I was then sent forth to find a photographer and of course the second I showed my face I was greeted with an assortment of disapproving looks from the crowd. I was evidently the last person they wanted to see emerge from the tent. Anyway, the picture was taken just as ace Space Shuttle pilot Bob Crippen showed up and had to be coerced into the frame. Seconds later the show began and we all went to our places.

Bob Crippen, John Cameron, James Cameron, Alan Hale, George Whitesides, Frank Drake, Jim Lovell, Pascal Lee, Buzz Aldrin, Patrick Stewart, Frank Braun, Bill Paxton, Morgan Freeman, Jeff Setelle, Rick Tumlinson, Peter Barnett, Jeff Baxter, Robert Godwin and Dan Richter. For some unfathomable reason Tom Huckabee, the event director, managed to miss this moment.

The show began with the eye of HAL 9000 and the voice of Xander introducing Patrick who started with, *"This is a very historic event and we are honouring a man who has been a hero of mine since childhood, and a man who in the last few years, as a result of a certain obscure television series I was once associated with, became my friend."*

Patrick then invited Morgan Freeman to come out and regale us with a reading from *Rendezvous with Rama*. It was a great moment and we were all thrilled to hear that Mr. Freeman had optioned the book for a movie. (We're all still patiently waiting, Mr Freeman...) When asked later about Clarke he said, *"I read Rendezvous with Rama and it really got to me, and then I saw 2001. The way he visualises living in space, space travel, it's not like other people do, the theatrics are not for theatrics sake."*

Patrick Stewart listens intently to Morgan Freeman reading from
Rendezvous with Rama

Jim Lovell and Buzz Aldrin looking for a monolith

Buzz and Jim Lovell came out next and toasted Arthur and told stories of their Gemini mission together. Lovell said, "*Arthur Clarke was really one of the early pioneers, I guess his future and his visions of what space would be like were part of the stepping stones that made us go into space, that made Buzz and I do Gemini 12. And then of course on Apollo 8 when I first saw earth as it really was on that very first flight. I kept thinking about 2001 and would I see that monolith down there!*" Buzz Aldrin then followed with, "*He's very insightful with a great sense of humour. He is like science itself. A candle in the dark. His writing is clear and thought provoking. He really challenges a person to cast aside the fantasy in science fiction and pick up the reality.*"

It was Jim Cameron's turn next and he spoke earnestly (for twice his allotted time) about how 2001 and Arthur had been one of the main influences on his life. *"We are now living in a world predicted by Arthur and the other great sf authors. Our reality today is the stuff of their dreams of 40-50 years ago. Arthur showed us the future and continues to do so with his fiction. It'll be centuries before reality catches up with his most advanced visions, but he opens a door and he shows us the way."*

James Cameron acknowledges that Arthur is in fact the King.

Unbeknownst to Cameron and most of the other people in attendance one of those fangled communications satellites was sitting on standby in the Clarke orbit awaiting a summons from our technical director. The stage had two identical podiums. Up to this point the one on the right had stood vacant but things were about to happen and I think I was one of only a very few people who knew exactly what was coming. I begged my guests to excuse me and I made my way forward into the middle of the dining crowd wielding my small camera.

Fred Clarke takes the witness stand and introduces his brother

Next Fred Clarke stepped up to the left podium and for a brief moment it seemed as though Arthur had been cloned and was holding forth in person, although Fred was much more reserved and moved through the eye of his brother's storm like one of those unflappable tornado hunters. *"His work goes on and we intend that it shall for many years. Long after our input has finished,"* Fred predicted.

He then announced that the guest of honor was going to speak to us live via satellite from his home in Sri Lanka. The guests anticipated the usual thing; a disembodied voice coming out of the PA, or something like that. But what they didn't know was that a team from Teleportec, a company from Manchester in England, had worked their way around the world to Arthur's house in Sri Lanka while their counterparts were set up in the shadows around the Playboy gardens.

Space Station V - The Hilton Hotel floats and rotates above the podium

As though summoning a genie from a bottle Fred waved his hand at the podium to his left and a bright point of light appeared floating in thin air. It looked for all the world like Tinkerbell had just flown onto the stage. The audience suddenly went quiet and tried to assimilate what they were seeing, then in one breathtaking instant the floating firefly expanded into the magnificent Hilton hotel Space Station floating and rotating in free space above the podium. The audience collectively gasped (as did I) and then before they could draw breath the space station disappeared into a black hole and instantaneously expanded back into a beaming Arthur C. Clarke wearing a grey jacket and light blue shirt standing at the podium.

Rick Tumlinson of the Space Frontier Foundation chats with holographic Arthur.

It was the first public demonstration of a live, full colour hologram to be sent via satellite around the world. In an instant the whole crowd drew breath and then broke into wild applause and started chattering like children at a magic show. For the next fifteen minutes Patrick Stewart and then Rick Tumlinson of the Space Frontier Foundation held a lively conversation with Arthur as if they were standing side by side. The delay was almost imperceptible as though the space gods didn't dare impede a message from their very own Mercury. Frankly, it was a truly breathtaking sight and I defy anyone to think of a more appropriate first use of the technology. I snapped a few pictures, which seem to have been about the only decent shots anyone managed to take that night because everyone else was so completely sandbagged by what they were seeing. Arthur and Fred side by side. In keeping with this miracle of virtual reality Arthur played it for all it was worth, *"I'm delighted to be at this function and to hear my brother saying those nice things about me and all the other nice things the other people have said."* Exactly as though he was indeed in the room.

Patrick Stewart can't quite believe his eyes as he has a conversation with holographic Arthur who is actually 9300 miles away.

We all sat there mesmerized as the oracle of the orient cheerfully answered all the questions and smiled and nodded his head at the commendations pouring his way. Patrick Stewart asked Clarke if he had any advice for the audience as we moved into the new millennium. Clarke grinned and said, "*I think the best message I can give to anybody comes from the Hitchhiker's Guide to the Galaxy.... Don't panic!*" It was exactly the panacea people needed to hear, to lift the shadow of the preceding few weeks, and a roar of laughter permeated the crowd. Then it was all over. Arthur returned to his computer and we all jumped up and headed over to the hologram recording station which up to that point no had noticed set up at the back of the garden. Everyone then took it in turns to send a holographic message back to Sri Lanka where Arthur presumably got to experience all of our gushing praise in full 3D.

Later in the evening I made sure to chat with Fred Clarke who looked resplendent in his full tux and medals. A kind and gentle man if ever I met one. The evening gradually wound down and I finally made my way back to my wife who had been having such a great time I don't think she even noticed my absence. I told her that I had to take one look in the legendary Playboy grotto before we left. I don't know what I expected to see, the tales of debauchery were looming large; but nothing prepared me for the sight I encountered. Lying on one of the sun beds, smoking a cigarette was a completely exhausted ape-man who had been running around all night posing for pictures with people. As I came out of the grotto, laughing out loud, a somewhat bewildered looking Oliver Stone was wondering what was to be seen at the end of the long line of people. I didn't have the heart to tell him.

"Don't Panic!"

Fred Clarke stands in the bright spotlights of the holographic studio and sends a message to his brother.

Dan Richter intimidates everyone with Moonwatcher's bone

And so the *Beyond 2001* Gala ended. A resounding success and a fantastic tribute to the mighty mind who had brought us all together. To my dying day I will never forget that night and I am immensely proud to have played a role in it.

It seems to me that in the year 3001 if there are any of us still puttering around this planet they will be looking back on the third millennium and pondering what the world was like back in 2001. The name of Clarke will almost certainly enter the conversation. How could it not? Let's hope our descendants have built Arthur's interstellar spacecraft and have completely forgotten Orwell and are not still bumbling around and muttering "if only..."

Chapter XIII - Later Days

90th Birthday Reflections

by Arthur C. Clarke

Hello! This is Arthur Clarke, speaking to you from my home in Colombo, Sri Lanka. As I approach my 90th birthday, my friends are asking how it feels like, to have completed 90 orbits around the Sun. *Well, I actually don't feel a day older than 89!*

Of course, some things remind me that I have indeed qualified as a senior citizen. As Bob Hope once said: *"You know you're getting old, when the candles cost more than the cake!"*

I'm now perfectly happy to step aside and watch how things evolve. But there's also a sad side to living so long: most of my contemporaries and old friends have already departed. However, they have left behind many fond memories, for me to recall. I now spend a good part of my day dreaming of times past, present and future. As I try to survive on 15 hours' sleep a day, I have plenty of time to enjoy vivid dreams. Being completely wheel-chaired doesn't stop my mind from roaming the universe – on the contrary!

In my time I've been very fortunate to see many of my dreams come true! Growing up in the 1920s and 1930s, I never expected to see so much happen in the span of a few decades. We *"space cadets"* of the British Interplanetary Society spent all our spare time discussing space travel – but we didn't imagine that it lay in our own near future...

I still can't quite believe that we've just marked the 50th anniversary of the Space Age! We've accomplished a great deal in that time, but the 'Golden Age of Space' is only just beginning. After half a century of government-sponsored efforts, we are now witnessing the emergence of commercial space flight. Over the next 50 years, thousands of people will travel to Earth orbit – and then, to the Moon and beyond. Space travel – and space tourism – will one day become almost as commonplace as flying to exotic destinations on our own planet.

Things are also changing rapidly in many other areas of science and technology. To give just one example, the world's mobile phone coverage recently passed 50 per cent – or 3.3 billion subscriptions. This was achieved in just a little over a quarter century since the first cellular network was set up. The mobile phone has revolutionized human communications, and is turning humanity into an endlessly chattering global family! What does this mean for us as a species?

Communication technologies are necessary, but not sufficient, for us humans to get along with each other. This is why we still have many disputes and conflicts in the world. Technology tools help us to gather and disseminate information, but we also need qualities like tolerance and compassion to achieve greater understanding between peoples and nations.

I have great faith in optimism as a guiding principle, if only because it offers us the opportunity of creating a self-fulfilling prophecy. So I hope we've learnt something from the most barbaric century in history – the 20th. I would like to see us overcome our tribal divisions and begin to think and act as if we were one family. *That* would be real globalisation...

As I complete 90 orbits, I have no regrets and no more personal ambitions. But if I may be allowed just three wishes, they would be these.

Firstly, I would like to see some evidence of extra-terrestrial life. I have always believed that we are not alone in the universe. But we are still waiting for ETs to call us – or give us some kind of a sign. We have no way of guessing when this might happen – I hope sooner rather than later!

Secondly, I would like to see us kick our current addiction to oil, and adopt clean energy sources. For over a decade, I've been monitoring various new energy experiments, but they have yet to produce commercial scale results. Climate change has now added a new sense of urgency. Our civilisation depends on energy, but we can't allow oil and coal to slowly bake our planet...

The *third* wish is one closer to home. I've been living in Sri Lanka for 50 years – and half that time, I've been a sad witness to the bitter conflict that divides my adopted country.

I dearly wish to see lasting peace established in Sri Lanka as soon as possible. But I'm aware that peace cannot just be wished – it requires a great deal of hard work, courage and persistence.

I'm sometimes asked how I would like to be remembered. I've had a diverse career as a writer, underwater explorer, space promoter and science populariser. Of all these, I want to be remembered most as a writer – one who entertained readers, and, hopefully, stretched their imagination as well.

I find that another English writer – who, coincidentally, also spent most of his life in the East – has expressed it very well. So let me end with these words of Rudyard Kipling:

If I have given you delight
by aught that I have done.
Let me lie quiet in that night
which shall be yours anon;
And for the little, little span
the dead are borne in mind,
seek not to question other than,
the books I leave behind.

This is Arthur Clarke, saying Thank You and Goodbye from Colombo!

(The above interview was from text from a YouTube video address, running time: 9 mins 3 secs, recorded on 5 December 2007, and reproduced by kind permission of the Sir Arthur C. Clarke Estate and Colombo-based production company Video Image (Private) Limited, in collaboration with the non-profit educational media foundation TVE Asia Pacific.)

Arthur at 4 Blenheim Road, Minehead

Chapter XIV - Fred Clarke

by Mark Stewart

Very few of us are fortunate enough to go through life with a personal champion to help and support us at every turn. But Arthur C. Clarke was lucky enough to have such an advocate in his brother Fred. The two brothers have always reminded me of Jim Nightshade and Will Halloway – loyal and heroic friends – in Ray Bradbury's elegiac masterpiece Something Wicked This Way Comes: inseparable and devoted to each other. Where one goes, the other will always follow: "The wind flew Jim away. A similar kite, Will swooped to follow."

Fred and Arthur shared a bond that not even half the Earth's circumference could break. When Arthur moved to Sri Lanka (or Ceylon as it was then known) in the 1950s, Fred stayed in the UK. They met up regularly thereafter at various events such as the Minehead Space Festival in 1992 (recently revisited on the BIS website), and always it seemed as if the brothers had never been apart.

I had the privilege of meeting Fred only once but it was enough to be struck by his selfless devotion to the Clarke legacy. In his tales and anecdotes, Fred could evoke Arthur better than anyone. During that meeting it was as if the more famous of the two siblings was there in the same room, a benign presence warmly appreciative – as he always was – of his brother's efforts, of Fred's unfailing resolve not to let time diminish the intensity of Arthur's achievements. And surely those achievements are, in part at least, also Fred's. After all, he was the one who got out of bed in the early hours of the morning to answer the phone to Stanley Kubrick when the famously demanding auteur wanted to speak to Arthur. And that was just one instance among countless others when Fred was the first to step forward in his brother's name, the first to champion his work.

What struck me most about Fred was his ability to deal with the adversities of advancing years in good cheer. In that respect he was one of the bravest men I have ever encountered. Problems with mobility and failing eyesight did nothing to dampen his enthusiasm and energy. In many ways, he was much like Reg Turnill, another champion now sadly lost to us. With the recent departure of Patrick Moore and Les Shepherd it really does seem as if the early history of the BIS is passing beyond living memory; but not beyond the Society's ability to record the vital contribution these individuals made to its history and its legacy. We were lucky indeed to have Fred in our ranks (an exemplar of Shakespeare's "good yeoman", and none better) supporting the BIS for as long as he did, progressing from a founding figure to a much loved elder statesman.

By all accounts, Fred was an unfailingly modest man, never fazed by the glamour that surrounded his brother. To paraphrase Kipling, he walked "with Kings" but never lost "the common touch." Occupying neither the spotlight nor the shadows, he was always a distinctive figure, standing by his brother's side, a position he maintained from childhood to the last of his days, tirelessly working to the very end to keep Arthur's memory alive. He was the brother we might all have wished for. And like Arthur, Fred was a man of letters, the author of several books.

I'd like to think the brothers, separated by Arthur's death in 2008, are together again now, perhaps somehow back in the fields surrounding the family farm in Somerset: two kites swooping together; two kestrels on the wing, both chasing once more the dreams they were destined to share in life.

Chapter XV - Fictional Last Word

The two boys made their way across the field – one of countless such fields that covered the Somerset countryside in an irregular patchwork in 1930 – heading towards the old farmhouse where they lived. They were thin but healthy lads, country boys both, one thirteen, and the other nine. Behind them the Sun was already withdrawing its light, though the air was still bright and warm.

"You know, Fred," said the older boy, *"the Sun is a star and there are millions of them out there. Billions even."* He waved his hand at the summer sky, a familiar preoccupied look on his face. *"Too many for the two of us to count, even if we live to be a hundred."* As yet the sky wasn't dark enough to show even the brightest of the constellations but he knew they were out there; he always knew. He never stopped thinking about space.

"I know that, Arthur," the boy called Fred replied. *"You've told me often enough. And you spend long enough staring at 'em through that telescope of yours."* There was a trace of exasperation in his voice but mostly it held affection and admiration.

"Maybe one day I'll travel to one of those Suns, in a spaceship," said the young stargazer. It was an outlandish claim spoken matter of factly, as though it were the most plausible thing in the world: a dream of interstellar flight on a planet that had yet to send a single rocket into orbit.

"I wouldn't be surprised if you did, Arthur. I wouldn't be surprised at all."

After a moment the younger boy asked: *"Will you take me along, if you do go?"*

"Of course," replied the would-be space cadet, responding without hesitation. *"We're brothers aren't we? We'll always be together."* He looked at his companion, his gaze holding a familiar challenge. *"Race you back to the house!"*

And the two boys, swooping and darting like kestrels, raced each other back home, heading towards a shared future as bright and as timeless as the setting Sun.

• • • • • • •

Resources and Recommended Reading

1. The Arthur C. Clarke Foundation: www.clarkefoundation.org

2. The British Interplanetary Society: http://www.bis-space.com

3. Icarus Interstellar: http://www.icarusinterstellar.org

4. Institute for Interstellar Studies: http://www.I4IS.org

5. Odyssey – the authorised biography of Arthur C. Clarke, by Neil McAleer, Published by Gollancz, 1992; and subsequently revised and expanded in Visionary: the Odyssey of Sir Arthur C. Clarke, now available through the Arthur C. Clarke Foundation.

6. Astounding Days, by Arthur C. Clarke, Published by Gollancz Paperbacks, 1990.

7. Ascent to Orbit, The Technical Writings of Arthur C. Clarke, A Scientific Biography, Wiley, 1984.

8. 2001: the Lost Science by Adam Johnson, Apogee Prime, 2012

9. Rob Hansen's Early British Science Fiction archive http://www.fiawol.org.uk.

10. The numerous science and science fiction books that Arthur left behind.

Selected Papers by Arthur C. Clarke

"Science Discussions and Brass Tacks", May 1938 issue of Astounding Science-Fiction

"An Elementary Mathematical Approach to Astronautics" JBIS, January 1939

"Linearity Circuits" pp.256-266, Wireless Engineering, June 1944

"The Astronomer's New Weapons, Electronic Aids to Astronomy" August 1945, volume 55, no.6, pp.43-147, Journal of the British Astronomical Association

"Extraterrestrial Relays" October, 1945 Wireless World, pp.305-308

"The Rocket and the Future of Warfare" March 1946, pp.61-69, Royal Air Force Quarterly

"Astronomical Radar" October 1946, Wireless World

"A Universal Escape-Velocity Mass-Ratio Chart" May 1947, vol.2, no.4, pp.72-73, Bulletin of the British Interplanetary Society

"More Television Waveforms" November 1947, pp.245-247 Electronic Engineering

"Stationary Orbits" December 1947, Vol.57, no.6, pp.232-237, the Journal of the British Astronomical Association

"Electronics and Space-Flight" March 1948, vol.7, no.2, pp.49, 69, JBIS

"Principles of Rocket Flight Part 1 – The Laws of Rocket Motion January 1949, pp.14-16, The Aeroplane

"Principles of Rocket Flight Part 2 – The Rocket Flight in Space" January 1949, pp.48-50, The Aeroplane

"The Dynamics of Space-Flight" March 1949, vol.8, no.2, pp.71-84, JBIS

"The Radio Telescope" April 1949, Vol.59, no.5, pp.156-159, the Journal of the British Astronomical Association

"Electromagnetic Launching As a Major Contribution to Space-Fight" November 1950, JBIS, vol.9, no.6, pp.261-267

"The Rocket and the Future of Astronomy" 1952, vol.2, no.14, pp.127-136, Occasional Notes of the Royal Astronomical Society

"An Optimum Strategy for Interstellar Robot Probes" November 1978, JBIS, Letter, vol.33, no.11, p.438

"The Space Elevator: 'Thought Experiment', or Key to the Universe?"1981, vol.1, no.1, pp.39-48, Advances in Earth Oriented Applications of Space Technology

• • • • • •

About the Authors

Mark Stewart, Fred Clarke, Kelvin F. Long

Fred Clarke is an author and the founder of the Rocket Publishing Company. In his long career he has also been a heating engineer. He is a Fellow of The British Interplanetary Society and a great advocate for manned space exploration. He is also the brother and long-time supporter of Arthur C. Clarke.

Mark Stewart is a Fellow of the BIS. He is the Society's Honorary Archival Librarian and editor of the BIS monthly e-magazine, *Odyssey*. A life-long "space cadet" he has been reading Arthur's novels since the age of twelve and is now fast approaching his mid-century. Mark is a regular contributor to *Spaceflight* magazine and helps maintain the Society's own modest "Clarkives." He hopes that his children will one day see the genuine commercialisation of space, making Arthur's dream of shuttles to orbital space stations and the Moon a reality for all.

Kelvin F. Long is a physicist, aerospace engineer and author. He is a Fellow of The British Interplanetary Society, Secretary of the Technical Committee and is Chief Editor to the in–house technical journal, JBIS. He is dedicated to an optimistic vision for humanity in space inspired by the writing of Sir Arthur C. Clarke. He is the Director of the Institute for Interstellar Studies.

Robert Godwin and Fred Clarke
at the Beyond 2001 gala in Los Angeles November 2001.

Robert Godwin is the owner and founder of Apogee Space Books. He is also the Space Curator at the Canadian Air & Space Museum. He has written or edited over 150 books including the award winning series "The NASA Mission Reports". Robert has appeared on hundreds of radio and television programs in Canada, the USA and England. He co-sponsored the event *Beyond 2001 – The Arthur C. Clarke Gala* at the Playboy Mansion in November 2001 and most recently co-produced with Michael Lennick the TV documentary *2001 – The Science of Futures Past.*

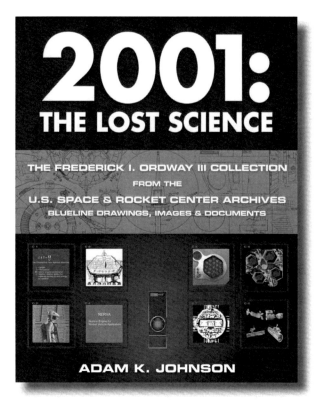

Odyssey – the bridge between imagination and reality

The British Interplanetary Society's monthly e-magazine, Odyssey, is devoted to the "imagination" component of the BIS motto, as well as to promoting its unique history and heritage. Within its electronic pages, readers will find interviews with today's leading writers of speculative fiction, as well as book and film reviews, and critical essays both on "hard "science fiction and key figures in the Society's history. Often featuring the graphic designs and artwork of Adrian Mann and David A. Hardy, Odyssey delivers a high visual and literary impact. The Odyssey portfolio includes regular essays and stories on the BIS website, and on the Society's Facebook page.

Odyssey offers you the chance to keep up to date with the latest Society news and events, and it's all at your fingertips. Another excellent reason to join the BIS!

Enquiries to the Editor, Mark Stewart, via mark.stewart@bis-space.com

The Journal of the British Interplanetary Society

First published in 1934, the Journal of the British Interplanetary Society (JBIS) was the first to describe many aspects of space travel which are now commonplace. After over 70 years of publication, JBIS is still concerned with originating and encouraging forward-looking ideas on how space exploration should develop. It is on the science citation index and is one of the highest rated astronautics journals in the world. JBIS is published monthly, and contains refereed academic papers from all over the world on all aspects of astronautics. This wide brief includes space science, space technology, spacecraft and space mission design, and humanities studies such as the philosophy of space flight. JBIS is available to British Interplanetary Society Members as either an alternative to Spaceflight magazine, or in addition, on payment of an additional discounted fee. Non-member and library subscriptions are available. Available from http://www.jbis.org.uk.

Spaceflight

Spaceflight is the international magazine of space. It first appeared in 1956, a year before the launch of Sputnik, and has been at the forefront of space exploration ever since. Spaceflight is published monthly with each volume of 12 issues having continuous pagination and an annual index included with the December issue. Widely used as a magazine of authoritative reference, Spaceflight has long been recognised as a prime source of information on international space programmes and commercial space exploration. Regular features, often written by those directly involved in a particular technology or project, cover all aspects of space technology and exploration, astronomy, satellites, commercial space, political activities, educational programmes and detailed space mission reports. Spaceflight is the ideal magazine for anyone professionally involved in the space business or for those with a general interest in the subject. Available from http://www.bis-space.com